BORN Bold

THE B.O.L.D. METHOD
How to Shatter Self Doubt and Unleash The Power Within

DR. ONAYSIA MARTINEZ

Born BOLD: The BOLD Method to Shatter Self-Doubt and Unleash the Power Within

© 2025 Dr. Onaysia Martinez. All rights reserved. No part of this publication may be reproduced, stored in a retrieval system, or transmitted in any form or by any means—electronic, mechanical, photocopying, recording, scanning, or otherwise—without prior written permission from the publisher, except in the case of brief quotations in critical articles and reviews.

For permissions and inquiries, contact:
The 1 and Only Publishing
4500 Forbes Blvd, Lanham, MD 20706
info@the1andonlypublishing.com
www.the1andonlypublishing.com

Luv U Gurl Media & Coaching LLC DBA Dr. Onaysia Martinez

Editing & Interior Design: The 1 and Only Publishing
Cover Design: The 1 and Only Publishing

Paperback ISBN: 979-8-89741-034-7.
Hardcover ISBN: 979-8-89741-036-1
Ebook ISBN: 979-8-89741-035-4

First edition. Printed in the United States of America.

Publisher's cataloging-in-publication data on file.

Scripture & References Notice

Scripture quotations are taken from the **Holy Bible, New International Version®, NIV®**. Copyright © 1973, 1978, 1984, 2011 by Biblica, Inc.™ Used by permission. All rights reserved worldwide.

Any brand names, product names, trademarks, service marks, or registered marks are the property of their respective owners and are used for identification purposes only. Unless otherwise noted, names and identifying details of individuals have been changed to protect privacy where appropriate.

The information in this book is provided for educational and inspirational purposes. The author and publisher make no guarantees and disclaim liability for any loss or risk, personal or otherwise, incurred as a consequence of the application of any information presented herein.

*To my sisters—Sarai, Chloe, and Gabriella—
may you never let the world silence your voice,
dim your light, or convince you to shrink.*

Contents

Intro: You're Already Her 1
Chapter One: Remember Your BOLD 11
Chapter Two: Don't Miss the Runway 23
Chapter Three: The Procrastination Prison 31
Chapter Four: The Readiness Trap 43
Chapter Five: Expand Your Impossible 53
Chapter Six: Dim No More 63
Chapter Seven: The Price of Maybe 77
Chapter Eight: Break Outdated Narratives 87
Chapter Nine: Own Your Vision 97
Chapter Ten: Lean Into Your Future Self 109
Chapter Eleven: When BOLDness Becomes A Burden 119
Chapter Twelve: Dominate, Take Action 131
Epilogue: Your BOLD Action Plan 143
Your Next BOLD Move 151
About the Author 153
Works Cited 155

Intro
YOU'RE ALREADY HER

My mother always said I was born bold. She loves telling the story of how I came out with a head full of hair and these big, brown eyes that let her know I was ready for the world.

Let's fast forward to 2005. Providence Place Mall, Rhode Island. We were in Warwick mall on Bald Hill Road on a Saturday afternoon. I was visiting my dad at his job—the local Foot Locker—walking around, checking out the latest pink and silver Skechers that had just dropped when my song came on. "Never Leave You (Uh Oh)." The beat began to stir up, and I felt it inside my bones.

The store was filled with folks asking for shoe sizes and employees running up and down the aisles to grab extra pairs from the back. My dad was assisting a customer with a sale. I didn't think. I just moved and let the music take me where it wanted to.

In a heartbeat, I jumped onto the shoe display platform in the center of the store. No mic, no dance rehearsal prepared. Just my love for music, bringing the party everywhere I go, and my passion for joy. At six-years-old, quite the porker, in my brown and yellow (yes, interesting choice) Catholic school uniform and my eight twisties with clear balls at the ends, I started my concerto.

"If you want me to staaaayyyy, I'll never leave," I sang to the tune, my beads clicking and clacking, my hips rocking and my hand waving in the air like Beyoncé's Single Ladies before it even was a thing. I didn't care who was in the room, what they would think of me, or even if I was singing on key. I just knew, right then and there, that I was free. Nobody could take the power I had away from me.

As I sang and danced, everyone stopped inquiring about the latest Jordans and began to form an audience.

"Woohoo! You go girl!" a woman with a pink Juicy sweatsuit cheered.

There was clapping and laughter filling the air. So much so that I felt as if I had been transported to Madison Square Garden. What most people would feel—fear, hesitancy, worry—I had only joy, freedom, and exhilaration. What was most interesting to note is that I never surprised myself. It was always like: This is who I am, this is me, how could I be any different?

If nobody else was going to do it, then I had to be the first. I had to be BOLD.

BORN *Bold*

I could not share this story without giving credit to my aunt, Titi Mino. She instilled in me that I could be confident, cute, and sassy, no matter how I looked or what people might think of me. She told me every day that I was "the shit," that I could do anything, and that I was "that girl." I thank God for her, as she inspired the daily boldness practices that I teach my clients today. But it was this reinforcement coupled with a deep, inner knowing of who God meant for me to be that, every time I got onto a stage, I was able to speak my mind. I took up space, I felt my heart explode with content.

That little girl? She's you, too. She's who you were before life taught you that dimming your light was safer than risking rejection. Before you became an expert at reading rooms and shrinking by the inches. Before you learned that acceptance meant making yourself smaller so others could stay comfortable.

There's a version of you that could change everything, but you've been playing small to keep everyone comfortable. You can command a room—on paper—but still second-guess the moment that room turns and waits for you to speak.

You're afraid to show up in your wholeness, because what if they don't accept all of you? What if your full power is too bright, too bold, too much for the spaces you've been trying to fit into?

Well, that's kind of a trick question. Because you're not "too much" of anything, and that version of you—that woman—lives within you right now. You're just in the middle ground between who you've been and who you're becoming. It's like as if you're a good student but you're trying to go from a B to an A+. You're already a good student by definition, but there's something missing. Something greater is calling you. And you can totally stay in the B realm, make do, and coast through, but it just won't feel like enough. And that voice will keep calling until you pick up the receiver.

YOU ALREADY ARE HER

That fearless woman lives within you right now. Boldness is your birthright. But you've been chasing this "better, more refined" version of yourself. When I say "better," I don't mean becoming someone different at your core. What I mean is for you to become more authentically you than you've ever been. Stepping into your next level isn't about changing locations or switching bodies like a warped version of Freaky Friday. It's about embracing your essence and having the courage to fully unfold every layer of who you truly are. For so long, you've been hiding her from the world. And because of that avoidance, she needs to be unlocked. She needs to be nourished. And she needs permission to take up space.

You are not broken. But the way society has been set up against you is. Your cultural upbringing has conditioned you. You've been taken for granted, misjudged, misunderstood, underestimated, and overlooked. But you have always been enough. You have always been everything you need to be. You have always had what it takes. You have always been BOLD. But somewhere along the way, your ability to unlock that power, that potential, that purpose, has been severed. And it's time we reestablish your connection.

Here's what every woman needs to know: BOLDness isn't about having enough confidence or being the loudest in the room. It's about taking ownership of your power in an instant. Whether you feel BOLD or not, it's a skill you can develop. It means casting your vision, believing in it deeply, and pursuing it despite obstacles. That's not just confidence—it's resilience. It's quantum-leaping into your future self instead of delaying the life you deserve.

This book will rewire everything you thought you knew. Your mind will be forever reprogrammed to do what it was meant to do: work for you, instead of against you. You'll see opportunities where you once saw obstacles. You'll trust your voice over everyone else's doubts. Every piece of your life will align just as it should. You'll walk into every room knowing you ARE one of one. You will start being in the driver seat of your life instead of just going along for the ride. And you will not be taking pit stops. You'll become unstoppable. That is a promise.

THE COST OF STAYING SMALL

Let's tell the truth: staying the same has a price tag. The invoice looks like generational patterns of women—especially women of color—making themselves smaller to survive systems that weren't built for us. Brilliant ideas stay locked in our heads while less qualified voices get the platform, the funding, the credit. Systemic suppression that continues because we've been conditioned to wait for permission instead of taking our seat at the table. Legacies that fade into "what could have been" instead of "this is what I built." A world that stays exactly the same because we choose safety over the impact we were assigned to make.

You don't need another year of "almost"s. You need a quarter of aligned Yeses and strategic Nos. You need to be a woman who moves with ease.

HOW TO USE THIS BOOK

This is a workbook and action-based guide. Each section helps you locate where you're stuck, release what's holding you back, and act—today. You'll see yourself in the scenarios; you'll hear your own internal monologue in the "traps." You'll get actionable steps, exercises, and tools you can use in business, leadership, relationships, and any other arena where your voice and choices matter. Every chapter ends with micro bold moves, because transformation doesn't happen in theory—it happens in the next five minutes. Expect invitations to post, pitch, price, ask, decline, delegate, or decide. Expect to feel your heart rate rise. That's your power waking up, not a warning to stop.

We'll unpack **The BOLD Method**™—the scaffolding you'll use to build on. **Break Outdated Narratives** interrupts the cycles of overthinking, perfectionism, and delay that keep you circling the block instead of exiting onto the highway. We use mindset rewiring, 24-hour decisions, and "fear-first" sequencing to move before your brain stalls you out. **Own the Vision** means naming what you actually want—not what's safe, expected, or applaudable. Declare a standard that scares you a little and excites you a lot. Translate desire into direction. **Lean Into Your Future Self** anchors to what she would do, how she would act, what habits she would create, and helps you connect to her so your moves aren't doubted or judged in the now. **Dominate. Take Action.** Making the leap builds daily practices that make boldness your baseline—self-trust reps, visibility reps, boundary reps. You'll have everything you need to take BOLD action; relentlessly.

Whether you're negotiating a contract, launching an offer, changing careers, leaving a good situation for a great one, or finally telling the truth about what you want... **The BOLD Method**™ moves you from concept to courage to consistency.

Before we begin, anchor your intent. Copy this into your notes, sign it, date it, and—if you're feeling extra BOLD—say it out loud:

"I am already BOLD. I refuse to postpone the life I was destined to live. I will act before fear gets a vote. I will protect my vision, my standards, and my energy. I will become easy to move and impossible to derail. I will not negotiate with smallness—mine or anyone else's. I will measure momentum, not perfection. Starting now."

VISION-MAPPING EXERCISE

Here's how we're going to start building the life of your dreams. What is your five-year plan? What goals do you want to accomplish? What does your life look like?

Create a vision board either on paper—using magazine cut-outs (the old school way) or printouts—or use a simple tool like Canva to do a digital one. Create statements in the present such as, "I'm a millionaire" as if it has already happened. Now, what would it take for this five-year plan to happen in three years? A year? Six months? Write down everything you would have to do. Then start with one thing on your list.

> **PRO TIP:**
> Head to www.bornboldbook.com for a FREE vision board template.

THE MOUNTAIN VISUALIZATION

Close your eyes and take three deep breaths. Picture yourself standing on the peak of a mountain, looking down at a vast landscape below. In this landscape, you can see all your current goals and aspirations—but here's the key—you're seeing them as already accomplished.

You've built the business. You've made the impact. You've stepped into the fullness of who you were meant to be. From this elevated perspective, feel the power flowing through your body, the deep resilience in your bones, the unshakeable knowing that you are exactly who you need to be.

This is your energy. This is your power. This is who you already are. Stay in this feeling as you continue reading this book. When doubt creeps in, when fear tries to negotiate you down, return to this mountain. Remember: this space—this powerful, resilient, unstoppable version of you—is always available. You're not trying to become her. She is you; you're remembering her.

Because you were given this vision for a reason. You were given this life for a reason. You are on an assignment, and it is unique to you, so you can't expect others to fulfill it for you. You are the CEO. You are the one in charge. You have been for a while now. But the longer you wait to make use of the power you withhold, the longer your legacy is pushed back, the greater the chance that it will never come to be.

We begin now.

Chapter One
REMEMBER YOUR BOLD

Right now, as you're reading this, there's a boardroom somewhere where a woman just edited her game-changing idea down to a "small suggestion." There's a Zoom screen where someone's camera is off because she's not sure her face belongs in that particular rectangle today. There's a draft folder where a world-shifting offer is collecting digital dust because it's not "polished enough" yet. There's an entrepreneur sitting on a pricing strategy that would double her revenue because she's scared to charge what she's worth. There's a woman with a revolutionary course idea that stays in her head because she's waiting for the "right time" to launch.

And there's you—brilliant, accomplished, tired of playing small, and wondering why taking up the space you were designed for still feels like asking for too much.

Before we go anywhere, I want you to hear me: I see the knot in your stomach when you picture Saying the Thing out loud. I see the questions that won't quit— What if I mess this up? What if I look foolish? What if it actually works and I can't carry it? You're not broken. You're not behind. You learned to make yourself smaller to keep the room calm. That's not weakness—that's survival.

Exhale. You're safe here.

Now, let me go first. I'll put my story on the table so you can borrow my courage until yours wakes back up.

Back when I was in college, I was in the 3+3 doctoral program for Physical Therapy. I had signed up during my junior year of high school, way before I even knew what physical therapy was. I didn't have a role model to look to. My mom got her degrees through weekend and summer programs. This was unknown territory. Any time I told someone my major, their response came fast: "Wow, that's hard. Most people fail and end up in Public Health." Gee, thanks for the input.

Nevertheless, I was fully committed.

What I came to find was this: people didn't lack ability. They lacked the desire to hold themselves to a higher standard—afraid they couldn't live up to it or, even scarier, that they'd become unrecognizable once they got there. If we're being honest, that's exactly what's been holding you back from your next level. Maybe it isn't a major anymore—you've long outgrown those decisions—but there is an area you've wanted to go further in. Business. Your career. Relationships. Community work. Your creative gifts. You've been avoiding the stretch because you, too, are afraid to fail, to disappoint, or to even be seen trying.

This is the only difference between the ones who run the table and the ones who keep circling it: not talent, not luck—the willingness to meet a higher standard and let yourself become the woman who can carry it.

In my second year of college, I had signed up to be a senior resident advisor, a role that most people didn't want because it came with a hell of a lot of responsibility, a role to uphold, and rules to regulate. People told me, "You won't be able to have fun." "You'll give up your weekends." "You can't balance between PT and anything else." But they also neglected to mention that you would also get free room and board, a beautiful resume, and a host of connections for future opportunities. These are things people in high places keep from us, women of color. They don't mention there are opportunities and ways in which you can climb to higher heights in life; to get ahead without necessarily cheating, but by seizing opportunity. By giving up a few of my weekends, I received $7,500 back into my pocket each semester.

I learned that opportunity meant access. But I had to go out and seek this opportunity, ask the right questions, and be willing to go where others couldn't in order to get to where I wanted to be. I couldn't just wait around for somebody else to do it for me. I had to block out what others told me, deflect their negative thoughts and opinions, and remain focused on my vision at all times.

I was asked to bring back an organization that had been absolute for years: the Latin American Student Organization (LASO). Alicia, my admirable mentor and advisor, asked me to do what nobody else could: provide a voice for Latinx students on campus and breathe life into a dying cause.

In just a year, LASO became the talk of the school. Through this work—re-founding LASO, holding a Senior Advisor role, and being president of two other organizations—I received so many scholarships that I was able to graduate with <$20,000 in debt. I did so much that I received the Chester McGuire Award of Leadership and Excellence, the highest distinction of leadership a student can receive. Because I moved beyond my fears and the doubt others instilled in my brain, I had saved hundreds of thousands of dollars. I received further opportunity, and I had advanced forward in my life at a young age. Imagine if I would have said, "Nah, I'll let someone else handle it."

BRING IT BACK

You have to be able to see yourself in a new light, a new role, a new status. This isn't about becoming someone new. It's about remembering who you were before the world told you who you had to be. Before you learned that the unknown was dangerous. Before you avoided new opportunities like the plague. Because here's what I know: that fearless woman who never questioned whether she "could?" She's still in there. And it's time to call her forward.

Born Bold

You don't need to become courageous—you need to collect the evidence that you already are. Right now, your brain is probably cycling through all the reasons why you're not BOLD enough, ready enough, equipped enough. Your brain is lying. You have receipts of your own courage scattered throughout your life, but you've been too busy apologizing for your power to gather them up and use them, on purpose.

Think back to the first time you said No and meant it, and your world didn't collapse. The night you asked for the raise, the date, the meeting, the referral—and lived to tell about it. The day you launched anything—and survived the awkward silence after hitting "publish." The moment you advocated fiercely for your kid, your team, your client, your own health. The hour you hit "send" on something that mattered, heart pounding, hands steady. None of these moments were accidents. They are data points from a nervous system that can absolutely move under pressure. You don't need a personality transplant. You need to remember your BOLD and use it on demand the next time your brain tries to negotiate you down to a smaller size.

"If I've done it before, I can do it bolder, better, and faster." That's your new mantra.

We didn't start with strategy for a reason. Strategy built on amnesia is just an expensive treadmill—you'll work hard, sweat impressively, and stay exactly where you started. Remembering your BOLDness is foundational because it changes what you believe is available to you. When you know you've done hard things before, hard things stop feeling impossible. When you have receipts of your own courage, courage stops feeling like something you need to borrow from someone else.

From this point forward, the play is beautifully simple: Remember. Call to mind a receipt. Decide. Choose a clean next step. Move. Do it before fear gets a vote. Everything else in this book supports that rhythm, but for now, we're restoring your baseline—the foundation from which all BOLD moves are made.

YOUR BRAIN IS KEEPING YOU ALIVE, BUT SMALL

You're not flawed. Your brain was built to keep you alive—not legendary. It remembers every embarrassing moment because evolution wired it to zero in on mistakes. Those mental replays? They're survival alerts, not commentary on your worth or potential. Your nervous system is fighting the bigger version of you.

The good news? You can lead your system through the resistance. We'll build skills that smooth the path: clean decision-making; swift, aligned action; and resilience after the leap, so you don't backslide the second the victory high fades.

You've got this. Trust me.

You are not "working on confidence." You are building self-trust. Confidence is what shows up after you've moved consistently—it's a trailing indicator. Action is the leading one, and action is always available to you. One daily decision that moves money, momentum, or meaning forward. One weekly ask that stretches your comfort zone by exactly one inch. One monthly visibility move that turns private excellence into public evidence.

Some people loved you smaller. They will not throw a parade for the version of you who refuses to shrink. That doesn't mean you're in the wrong—it means you're growing. Developing. Blossoming.

Your assignment is to learn how to distinguish between feedback that sharpens and feedback that holds you back. We keep the first. We release the latter with grace and without explanation. This is where you anchor deep into your faith: your assignment outranks their discomfort. Your calling wasn't designed by other people, and it doesn't require a unanimous vote to be stamped for approval.

EXERCISE: COURAGE COLLECTION

It's time to gather the evidence that you've always been BOLD, even when you forgot. We're building your personal anti-imposter dossier that you can return to every time your brain tries to convince you that you're not ready.

Part 1: Childhood Power Recall

Think back to your childhood. When you didn't think, you just acted. What did you have to do in order to overcome your fears? Did any of your fears come to be? Write about that time where you felt most powerful.

You did something you were proud of. You overcame a difficult obstacle.

Put on the song that makes you feel like you could run the world. You know the one. Stand somewhere that feels like a stage—your kitchen island, your office, the front steps of your house. Ask yourself: When was the last time I moved without asking permission? What did my body feel like right before I chose courage over comfort? Whose voice told me I was "too much," and when did I start believing them?

Now write three moments when you were undeniably, unapologetically YOU. Write them like scenes—include the sounds, the feelings, the exact moment you chose to move anyway. Give each story a power word: Spoke. Claimed. Launched. Left. Asked. Built. Put those words where you'll see them daily. They're not just memories—they're receipts.

Part 2: Negativity Audit

Write down all the negativity you faced when traveling down a road less traveled. What was the reward at the end? Think of this when you're onto your next chapter in life. Remember, stay focused and your opportunities will flourish.

You can channel your own fearless moments by active visualization techniques. Deep breathing. Calm environment. Reflect back to a time you felt most powerful. Your body remembers what it feels like to be whole. We're about to remind it.

Part 3: Your CEO Vault

As brilliant women, we so often forget all that we've accomplished because the world wants us to feel small and powerless.

Not on my watch. It's time you create a running list on your phone, titled "Receipts." For each entry, capture:

- Action—What exactly did I do?
- Friction—What almost stopped me?
- Result—What shifted (externally or internally)?
- Replication—Where can I use this same energy this week?

This ledger becomes your personal anti-imposter dossier. Read it before big asks. Read it after brutal days. Read it when the room goes cold and you need to remember you belong there.

You've been BOLD before. You are BOLD now. You'll be her again—starting in the next five minutes. The revolution begins with remembering.

> **PRO TIP:**
> Head to www.bornboldbook.com for access to the workbook to follow along in real-time.

KEY TAKEAWAYS:

- You were born BOLD—society conditioned it out of you, but it's still there
- Confidence is a trailing metric that follows action, not a prerequisite
- "Becoming her" is remembering who you already are, not replacing yourself
- Your assignment outranks others' comfort levels
- Remembering who you already are is the foundation for all BOLD moves

REFLECTION QUESTIONS:

- What's one moment from your childhood when you acted without seeking permission or approval? How did it feel in your body?
- Which voices have been loudest in your head when making decisions—yours or others'? Name them specifically.
- What's one area of your life where you've been apologizing for your power instead of using it?
- If you had to gather three pieces of evidence that you're already courageous, what would they be?

Chapter Two
DON'T MISS THE RUNWAY

Now that you've remembered who you already are, let's address the elephant in the room: if you're already BOLD, what's been stopping you from acting like it? The answer lies in the sophisticated ways fear disguises itself as responsibility.

When I was younger, I used to love playing with Bratz dolls. You couldn't catch me dead with a Barbie doll. No way. My house was filled with Bratz dolls, cars, dollhouses. You name it, I had it. I would spend hours playing by myself, letting my imagination take me wherever I wanted to go. One of my favorite make-believe games to play was Fashionista. I had my dolls set up for the stage: the latest clear pumps, Juicy crop tops and leather skirts.

But my doll, Jade, just couldn't figure out what to walk out on the runway in. She tried on over a dozen fits and just couldn't make a decision. The crowd grew tired. My other dolls, Sasha, Dylan, and Chloe, fell asleep awaiting her arrival.

That's it. She missed her moment. The show went on without her, and by the time she FINALLY decided on a rhinestone mini dress with red heels and a jean handbag, she had missed her shot.

You see, you're not much different from my girl, Jade. That decision to set your own stage, go after the promotion, say the grand-all idea at a meeting, start the non-profit; it's fleeting. While others are acting, you're "researching." You're "waiting for the right time." You're being "thorough." But the show is going on—with or without you.

Always researching. Perfectionism causing delay. Meanwhile, opportunities slip by while you circle the same block over and over again.

We're done circling. It ends today, girl.

The #1 excuse given is, "I'm waiting until the right time or for things to settle down to focus on x, y, z." This false concept of the "right time" or "life settling down" is what's keeping you back from the exact kind of life you desire. A life of fulfillment, opportunity, cash, legacy, lasting impact—you get the picture. Because what is the "right time," really?

There is always going to be another wrench thrown your way. There is always going to be another thing you must conquer. Another obstacle. Another challenge. Maybe you get laid off from your job. Or business sales aren't going as you projected with your team. Or you decided to finally write that book you've been holding off on. Yet, the world doesn't stop moving for you. Your kids get older. Your family drama continues. Politics get uglier and wars get bloodier. Life will continue—with or without you. And once you stop resisting, or convincing yourself that better days are coming, then we can really start building the life of your dreams.

When an opportunity comes knocking the first time, answer it, trust in it, and step fully into it—even if you're not certain where it is going to take you. Take it from me. If I had just listened to the gracious women who disclosed an opportunity for me the first time, I would've saved A LOT of time, energy, and money.

There is no such thing as the perfect time. Start now anyway.

THE HIDDEN COST OF CERTAINTY

That hesitation didn't just cost me convenience—it cost me my peace, my birthday celebration, and three days of my life I'll never get back. But more than that, it demonstrated how I was showing up everywhere else in my life. How many times had I stayed in line, convinced that patience would be rewarded, while opportunities passed me by?

This might be what you're experiencing right now—standing in metaphorical lines that aren't moving, while opportunities pass by. Overthinking and self-doubt aren't character flaws—they're learned responses among high-achieving women who've been conditioned to be thorough, to research extensively, to wait for ideal conditions that rarely arrive. You've been taught that being cautious is responsible, that listening to others' direction is wise, but what if I told you it's actually the exact thing that's keeping you small?

When your nervous system senses risk, it will present delay as wisdom. It's not. It's just a prettier cage. You've been conditioned to be careful, agreeable, uberprepared. You've been taught that safety and security come externally instead of internally. That conditioning, plus an overprotective brain, is built for safety, not success. And it leads to constant cycles of overthinking, perfectionism, analysis paralysis, hesitating.

Here are the most common masks procrastination wears when it targets ambitious women:

- The Over-Analyzer—three courses deep into something you could learn by doing for a week.
- The Perfectionist—editing a caption for 45 minutes that could have been posted in five.
- The People Pleaser—you ask five smart friends and borrow all their doubts.
- Pro tip: Take the quiz to find out which one you are at www.bornboldbook.com.

EXERCISE: HAVE A YES DAY

Whatever opportunity comes your way, an offer from a friend to go to a concert, an invite from your family to finally visit your aunt in North Dakota, whatever it is. Say YES to everything for one day without planning or delaying and see how magically your life unfolds.

Make the commitment. Take the leap. Then navigate the three predictable phases with your evolved identity as a guide:

- The High—adrenaline hits. Your heart is racing. You're filled with exhilaration and optimism.
- The Dread—after the Yes, energy crashes. You'll want to numb or do busywork. Your future self takes a 10-minute walk and sticks to the course.
- The Stretch—visibility, capacity, receiving. This is the widening. Your future self tracks receipts: what went right, what you learned, what you'll do again.

Your job isn't to "feel ready." It's to move as the woman who embodies your desired outcome while your current system catches up.

KEY TAKEAWAYS:
- Opportunities have expiration dates
- Your first instinct is often right—trust it before polling everyone else
- Hesitation costs more than imperfect action in most cases
- The "right time" is a myth that keeps you perpetually waiting
- Speed over perfection—others act while you analyze

REFLECTION QUESTIONS:

- What opportunity did someone else take while you were "thinking about it?"
- When was the last time you listened to your first instinct and it turned out to be right? What does this tell you about trusting yourself?
- What's one decision you're currently circling around that you already know the answer to?
- If you had to say Yes to something today without researching it to death, what would it be?

Chapter Three
THE PROCRASTINATION PRISON

This chapter is your jailbreak. We're going to expose the designer disguises procrastination wears when it targets high-achievers—research, polish, perfect timing—then replace it with moves that make speed your tried-and-true lover and action your go-to. Because the #1 reason powerful women stall isn't a lack of talent; it's that procrastination and overthinking are acting falsely as responsibility and maturity.

VICTIMIZATION IS YOUR ENEMY
"I don't have the same opportunity as others who don't look like me or weren't raised like I was." But here's where your power lives: in deciding what you'll do about it.

"I'm too old to start my business and get onto the tech wagon." The real question becomes: how will you close that gap?

"In this economy, it doesn't make sense to bet on me. So many bad things can happen." And when challenges arise—because they will—what's your strategy to navigate them?

Here's the shift that changes everything: when you move from focusing on external barriers to owning your response to them, you reclaim your power in the situation.

Yes, the world is crazy. Yes, your goals are big and audacious, yes, it's risky to bet on you. But if you don't, who will? No, honestly ask yourself. "If I don't bet on me, if I don't go after this speaking gig, if I don't raise my prices, if I don't sign this lease, who will bring my vision to life? Who will leave this legacy for my children? Who will make the difference in this world that God is calling me to do?"

The answer is simple: nobody will. Nobody is coming to save you. Nobody is coming to fill your shoes or take your spot in line. You and God are alone in this walk. So it's time you own up to your power. It's time to own up to your BOLD.

You have two paths available: you can continue to minimize the power stirring within you, or you can choose to acknowledge and step into that power. When you recognize your ability to influence your circumstances, you shift from feeling powerless to taking purposeful action. I'm sharing this directly because I see your potential, and I know you're capable of so much more. I know you've had things happen to you in life where you felt powerless, unsure how you would move forward. But. You. Did. And you're here today. That power to move on? That power has never left you. That is your BOLDness, you were born with it, and it's time you protect it.

Now that you know how to harness your power, you also know how risky it is to let it go and give it to someone else. You were given this vision for a reason. You were given this life for a reason. You are on an assignment and it is unique to you. So you can't expect others to fulfill it for you. You are the CEO. You are the one in charge. You have been for a while now. But the longer you wait on making use of the power you withhold, the longer your legacy is pushed back, and the greater the chance that it will never come to be.

UNCERTAINTY IS WASTING PRECIOUS TIME

I was at the airport one day, traveling home from a cruise to Aruba, Bonaire, and Curacao. My flight had gotten delayed while on the tarmac—one hour, then another, then another, and before I knew it it had already been four hours since we had been sitting on that tarmac waiting for permission to enter the JFK, NY airport after a travel ban was activated due to torment weather. There, four hours in, the flight attendants kindly ordered our butts off of the plane with nothing more than a "See customer service" as the next line of command. As we all moaned and groaned, threw on our carry ons and headed back into the dreadful airport terminal, I began seeking the next opportunity.

I headed to the customer service desk, the line wrapping around across the main hallway with a break incorporated for other travelers to pass through to their destinations. It was a long, nearly impossible line to overcome. The humidity from hundreds of frustrated bodies filled the air. People were arguing with gate agents, children were crying, and that pre-recorded voice kept announcing more delays in three languages. I could smell the stale coffee from the overpriced café mixing with stress, sweat, and recycled air conditioning.

As I stood at the back of the line, shifting my weight from foot to foot, my cruise tan already fading under the fluorescent lights, a woman who had just left the front of the line passed me. She was speaking to another passenger about how waiting in line was pointless.

I asked her, "You mean for the flight to NYC that was cancelled?"

"Yes, you're better off going on your phone. There's no one to talk to and they'll just tell you to call someone or go online," she retorted. "Good luck," were her last words.

I grew envious at the fact that she had escaped this windy, serpent-like line that hadn't moved an inch since I arrived. But through my uncertainty, I decided to stick to my original plan and wait in line as I was told. Something about being in line felt productive, like I was "doing something" by listening to what the authority—the clueless flight attendant—directed me to do.

Hours and hours, I waited in that line. 10 hours spent in the airport already, including the layover. I was restless, dehydrated, and exhausted. My back ached from standing. My phone was dying. I watched person after person get to the front, only to be told the same thing that woman had warned me about.

Another woman in front of me told me she got another flight while on the phone with a customer service agent. She then hopped out of line and into freedom, rolling her suitcase past all of us still stuck in place. Finally, I decided to take matters into my own hands. I decided to go onto my phone, remembering what that first woman said, and went onto the airline app.

To my dismay, all of the flights within the next 48 hours were booked. Taken by others who decided to take action and go against the current! Impossible! I pulled up a chat with an agent to see if there was anything they could do, flights to JFK, LGA, Boston, Providence—anywhere, at this point! I just wanted to get home. There was nothing, so as I stood in that line, just a couple feet from where I had originally started this unproductive journey, I booked a flight to JFK for 8 a.m. the following Tuesday. (It was Sunday).

I trotted out of the never-ending line, sad, and disappointed that I had not taken the opportunity that first woman had given me. I chose to stick with my own stubbornness because of my uncertainty and lack of trust in her own advice. This cost me 13 hours total in the airport; with no hotel accommodations; 48 total hours wasted in Hollywood, Florida; and a really crappy 26th birthday.

We're using the first letter of **The BOLD Method**™ to neutralize this trap. **Breaking outdated narratives** means filtering out what thoughts or beliefs you were conditioned to accept and giving them back to the original owner. Return to sender, you're not needed here!

Think about it, as a child you always acted on instinct, intuition, self trust. Until someone told you, "Think before you speak," "Be careful," "Don't take risks," and then you started delaying decisions that didn't have the approval stamp of your best friend, mom, great-aunt Susie, and your coworker who honestly couldn't care less.

Procrastination delays the negative feeling of discomfort and dis-ease. But that exact feeling is what you need to walk into. It's a requirement for growth. You cannot surpass it, but you can stop delaying it and choose to simply rip off the Band-Aid.

LANGUAGE TO BORROW WHEN YOUR BRAIN TRIES TO STALL:

When perfectionism kicks in: "This is a fast draft—sending it now, perfecting it as I go."

When you're overthinking the ask: "One sentence, one link, one date. Sending."

When fear tries to negotiate: "I don't need to feel ready to do what my heart tells me."

When the timeline feels wrong: "The right time is a myth. I don't know if I'll have tomorrow."

When you want to research more: "I can learn by doing and adjusting as I go."

When committee syndrome hits: "I'm not taking a vote on my vision. It is set in stone."

You don't "become confident" and then act. You act, and confidence follows. This is why we built it into the foundation: action generates confidence; confidence follows. We move first. We learn, refine, and move again. So today, we'll prove that your results don't depend on a perfect strategy. They depend on a willing spirit to take the right next step.

Perfectionism whispers that you're protecting excellence. You're not. You're protecting ego—the part of you that would rather stay unseen than risk being seen before you're pristine. Excellence comes from BOLD action, not delayed first attempts. Opportunities expire while you "think on it." Translate thinking into trying.

This isn't sloppiness; it's smart sequencing. Visibility, then refinement. When you model rapid, aligned decisions, you give permission for others to do the same. You create a chain reaction that sparks genius and ingenuity. You become comfortable with discomfort. People look up to you, even if they won't admit it yet. They wish they had your guts—and your clients from that launch.

Perfectionism is a tax. If you spend five times longer polishing, you pay with lost timing and expired opportunities. While you "think on it," opportunities pass on over to someone else. So we flip the math. Act fast, learn fast, adjust faster.

I'm not minimizing life's complexity. I'm calling out its expectancy. There will always be layoffs, school closings, market drops, politics, and scary headlines. Life keeps moving whether you decide to move or don't. You and God will walk this assignment—not the people in the back with their unsolicited opinions. So we do what BOLD women do: we move alongside reality. We move with ease. We make the first step and allow the rest of the staircase to appear. We become partners with fear and don't allow it to stop the ride, but invite it into the backseat.

> *Just after one session of talking to Dr. Martinez, she helped me shift my mindset in a way that I thought would never happen. She helped me realize that some things that you think are not achievable, they are. You just gotta push yourself forward and run after them. She helped me realize that I can basically combine my passion for travel and occupational therapy together to become a traveling occupational therapist.*
>
> *Not only did she do that, she showed me by leading by example, by seeing her go after what she wants and seeing her basically go into the unknown herself first. This inspired me to do the same by quitting my corporate job and finally doing what I love: traveling the world.*

> *With such boldness, she made me realize that I too can take a step into the unknown in not just my career, but in other aspects of my life. Dr. O, Thank you so much.*
>
> — Luna, previous client

EXERCISE: THE DREADED DECISION

Just like Luna did, make a decision you've been holding off on today. Not tomorrow, not next week, not when you have more information. Today. Pick the decision that's been circling in your mind for weeks or months. The one that makes your stomach flip when you think about it. The one you keep researching but never executing.

Set a timer for 2 hours. Within those 2 hours, make the decision and take the first, small actionable step. Send the email. Make the phone call. Submit the application. Book the consultation. Your future self is waiting.

Pro tip: Get your decision guide at www.bornboldbook.com for a full worksheet.

Close this chapter with one act that cracks your loop: Send the one-sentence ask. Post the beta offer with a pay link. Put the date on the calendar and invite the room. Exit the line you've been standing in and try the app. Have the difficult conversation you've been avoiding.

Speak up in the meeting instead of staying silent. Set the boundary that's been brewing in your mind for months.

Because the woman you're becoming doesn't wait for the weather to be perfect. She IS the weather. She brings about the storm within her. And when your brain tries to seduce you back into research, remember: this is how powerful women stay stuck. Be the first proof. When you move, the cycle shatters, and a new generation begins.

KEY TAKEAWAYS:
- Procrastination disguises itself as responsibility and thoroughness
- Victimization keeps your impact capped—take ownership of your timeline
- Pattern interrupts and 24-hour decisions break the overthinking loop
- Perfectionism is a tax that costs you timing and opportunities
- Every day spent overthinking is a day someone else spends doing

REFLECTION QUESTIONS:
- What story do you tell yourself that sounds responsible, but is actually fear keeping you from moving forward?
- Which mask does your procrastination wear most often—the Over-Analyzer, the Perfectionist, or the People Pleaser?

- What would you attempt this week if you stopped making your circumstances responsible for your timeline?
- Who benefits when you stay small and play it safe? (This question might surprise you.)

Chapter Four
THE READINESS TRAP

Breaking the procrastination loop is just step one. Now comes the part that separates the women who make subtle, temporary changes from the women who completely transform their lives: learning to move before you feel prepared.

It was a beautiful, sunny afternoon in May of 2023. I had just graduated with my doctorate in physical therapy. After six long years of late nights, cram sessions, and a TON of examinations, I finally did it! I was the one and only Latina in my graduating class, and my family was beaming with pride. We took photos, we partied, we did it all. But I wasn't done. Even after all of that hard work I put into this piece of paper, I still needed it to be stamped by the state of New York in order to receive my license to practice as an officially-registered physical therapist.

But I was tired. Exhausted. Brain was shot. Nothing left to give after those six gruesome years of vigorous study.

Some of my classmates had already taken the exam, and I felt the pressure on my back to sign up for the next registration date, just three months later, in July. Against my own feelings of exhaustion and fatigue, I closed my eyes and hit "Purchase" for a $1,000 ticket to my success. I enrolled in a test prep program that promised to get me my passing grade and gave me access to a cohort of hundreds of other students on the same path as me.

Week after week, I struggled to see myself as an actual physical therapist. Even after all of those late nights studying and practicing in the lab on campus, ordering pizza and jamming out to '90s R&B at 12 a.m., I was still not convinced. It was as if those long nights weren't nearly enough to give me permission to be what I'd worked so hard to become. I was studying, showing up, doing my assignments (sort of), and attending lectures. Then I started to slip. Not only was I exhausted, but I wasn't fully embodied with the identity of a physical therapist. But this was exactly what I needed in order to get to the next level: both the next level of my career and the next level of me.

I continued telling others I was studying, giving it my all, anticipating this day like it was the best day of my life. But inside? I was crumbling. Shaking. I wasn't certain about who Onaysia would be once she became responsible for other peoples' lives. The weight of that responsibility was almost unbearable. My chest would tighten every time I thought about it. My palms would sweat during practice questions. Would I mess up someone's knee and get sued? Would I lose my license over something stupid? Would I have to get rid of my nose ring to fit in with what a doctor "should" look like?

So many thoughts flooded through my head as the exam date started to approach. I felt like I was facing an ominous mountain that was so much larger than me, I couldn't even see the peak beyond the clouds. My head was murky, jaded, and quite frankly, over it. Fear loves an undefined future. It writes scripts and casts you as the understudy in your own life. The day finally came when the inevitable would occur. I had to show up, I had to take the exam, I had to expand my own horizons of self. But I wasn't ready. I wasn't even sure about the difference between a SLAP tear and an anterior impingement syndrome of the shoulder. I didn't know how many degrees of motion were normal in every single joint of the body. How dare I call myself a "real" therapist?!

But I honestly would have done fine without all of that. The truth is: I didn't know who I was when I entered that examination room. And I walked out letting the exam define me. Therefore, it defeated me. When I was faced with questions I didn't know, instead of honing in on my inner self trust and staying grounded, I was wavering in and out of confidence. I was answering them as the scared, uncertain student struggling and striving to pass her boards, not as the future physical therapist who would be able to execute them flawlessly.

I left that exam that day knowing I didn't have what it took. Knowing I wasn't ready to expand just yet. My fears had won that day. I ended up failing that exam, got 30 points shy of a passing grade. Proof that I wasn't too far off in my knowledge, I just didn't have a clear enough vision to hold onto. I couldn't see myself past my current self.

THE INNER VOICE

I spent two weeks crying, sulking, stricken with grief over what could have been. The shame was suffocating. I felt like I had let everyone down—my family, who had celebrated so proudly, my professors, who believed in me, and most importantly, myself. I questioned everything. Was this even meant for me? Had I been fooling myself this whole time? The voices in my head were relentless: You're not smart enough. You don't belong in this field. Everyone else can do this, but not you. I was ready to give up on this vision I had been instilled with for so long. Ready to throw in the towel.

Then I had to get real with myself. I hadn't truly done my best. Not because I couldn't, but because I wasn't fully invested in my decision that I would become a licensed physical therapist. Because I wasn't fully invested, when asked questions on the exam, I didn't answer them as a physical therapist. As my future self, who would know the answer without a doubt. I was answering them as the scared, uncertain student who was striving to become more.

I realized that I could hack this exam and become bigger than this mountain if I just saw myself as being the physical therapist who had passed already. I switched my entire approach. I started dressing as I would when I became a physical therapist daily, ditching sweats for khakis. Instead of being cooped up in my room, I started going out to cafes and libraries, meeting new people and telling them who I was going to be as if I was already there with pride and excitement. I started tackling practice questions from the lens of who I was becoming and not who I've always been. I started showing up differently—not halfway, but wholeheartedly.

I welcomed the fears. The voices. The self-doubt. I let them all sit at bay, and allowed abundance to flow into my consciousness and into my life. I was ready. It wasn't about the material I studied, it was about my own inner composition. Rewiring my very DNA to prepare to expand in a way that did not require a playbook. After three months of daily manifesting what it is I wanted, telling myself everyday that I am a physical therapist, acting as if I have already passed this exam, my thoughts turned to words, which became beliefs, and resulted in action that reflected that.

I walked into that next exam like the damn physical therapist who didn't even need to be there. She had already passed and surpassed those sitting in the room. She was confident, strutting, with a deep inner knowing of what would come out on the other side.

I passed that exam. Not only that, I aced it. Received nearly 300 points higher than my first try.

Once you set your mind to who you are, the world has a way of bowing down to your command, ready or not.

WHY WE RESIST EXPANSION

One could argue that I was more "ready" the first time I took that exam. But I wasn't. I just finally stopped resisting my expansion to the next level of my identity. I just let it be, I welcomed it, and stood, fully-assured, that I would end up okay on the other side.

Let's call out the ways you may be resisting expansion right now without even knowing it. I'll do it when life settles down. Life doesn't settle; you do. I just need more time to prepare. The more time you waste preparing, the less time you have to enjoy what you create. Let me wait until it's perfect. If I waited for perfection for my exam, I would have never taken it. I'm protecting my peace. Beautiful. But sometimes, "peace" is a padded cell where the loudest dreams go quiet. I don't want to be too much. Translation: I learned to make myself small to keep the room calm.

We're ending that today, queen.

Be kind to yourself—and be ruthless with the pattern. You are not flaky. You are not lazy. You're under-expanded for the life you keep asking for. And that is fixable.

Your brain evolved to prioritize safety—it's wired to detect threats and preserve you, not to propel you into uncharted greatness. In fact, when expansion asks for new capacity—whether that's time, money, visibility, or accepting help—the brain registers those unknowns as risks. That's why your nervous system can spin loops, offer compromises, and subtly steer you toward comfort zones.

But here's the hopeful part: through **neuroplasticity**, your brain learns by doing—by practicing new responses. Structured, repeatable experiences of gentle, yet consistent expansion—think small, incremental challenges with quick wins—can rewire your threat-response patterns. Over time, the flinch fades, your psychological space opens, and you grow into capacity you once deemed out of reach.

Understanding that readiness is a myth is just the first step. Now comes the harder question: What would you attempt if you gave yourself permission to dream beyond your current limitations?

EXERCISE: FUTURE-SELF FORMATION

Imagine yourself completing whatever challenge, aspiration, or goal you've been sitting on. Could be going after the raise or quitting the job altogether. Whatever it is for you, imagine the "you" you would be once you got there.

Now, spend time really bringing this person to life. What is she wearing? What is her demeanor like? How does she carry herself? Visualize it in your mind. Write it down. Now, tell yourself every morning that you are her already. And plan an action to do, big or small, that would align with your future self.

KEY TAKEAWAYS:
- "Ready" is a feeling you earn after the leap, not before it
- Your nervous system reads expansion as threat, even when it's growth
- The body learns by doing—action creates readiness, not the reverse
- Identity must shift before the title arrives
- Expansion requires new capacity for time, money, visibility, and receiving help

REFLECTION QUESTIONS:
- What's the difference between how you prepared for something you conquered versus something you avoided?
- When you imagine your boldest goal, what does your body tell you? Where do you feel excitement vs. fear?
- What would you start today if you accepted that you'll never feel completely ready for it?
- How has waiting for "the right time" actually cost you more than taking imperfect action would have?

Chapter Five
EXPAND YOUR IMPOSSIBLE

Once you stop waiting to feel ready, the real work begins: daring to envision a life bigger than anything your current environment taught you was possible.

SAY YES BEFORE YOU'RE READY

I help my coaching clients say Yes before they're ready simply by following my proven framework: **The BOLD Method**™. First, we focus on what voices and stories are telling you to hold off. Break outdated narratives. Then, once we can name what is holding you back, we get to work on the excavation process. We start to give back what you were told by family, society, and even yourself. Then we build evidence as to why those narratives are outdated or simply not true. As we build this evidence, or what I call a CEO Vault, your confidence begins to build and the outside voices get lower. And your voice? Much louder.

Then we work on improving your own internal voice through daily practices of self trust. Stating what you will do, even small actionable steps, and being committed to showing up for yourself. Then we get into Owning Your Vision. Mapping out what it is that you truly want, where you see yourself going, and comparing it to where you are now.

The secret is, this vision has to be so grand, so juicy, so powerfully made, that it trumps fear. If your vision is murky, muddy, or cloudy, this will not work. You have to be a visionary, you have to want to leave a legacy and leave your mark on this world. That vision, coupled with radical self-belief, is what gets my clients (and you) to take BOLD action. Without either or, there is no way to overcome fear and you will remain stuck.

Take it from LaDawn, a client who was in the educational field, looking to move into higher education with a focus on diversity and inclusion. She wanted to go after a position she felt was way above her experience and skillset. After working through **The BOLD Method**™ together, specifically Owning Her Vision, she was able to see her life and opportunity differently.

Before coaching with Dr. O, I wasn't entirely sure what my strengths were. I knew I was a strong individual, but I hadn't taken the time to look within myself to understand where I truly belonged or how to apply my strengths effectively. I had been sitting on the decision to pivot out of my career into a new, unprecedented space for a while but felt unqualified and uncertain. After going through this program, I gained the confidence and clarity to see why I was the best—and only—fit for the job. I discovered exactly who I am and developed the skills to position myself as valuable in any market and in my personal life. I walked into that room knowing I had it because I had already envisioned myself in the role. I couldn't have done it without Onaysia's program. Whenever I doubt myself, I will remind myself exactly who I am—that woman!

— LaDawn, previous client

FUTURE VS. FEAR

Here's the thing. I'm sure LaDawn was fearful prior to making her move into a bigger role and bigger paycheck. But her vision for her future conquering the DEI space was much vaster, larger, and wider than anything else. You, too, have to make the future so vivid and specific that it overcomes your fear. That is the power of **The BOLD Method**™. Vague desires cannot beat concrete fears. Fear will always win by default unless your vision is clearer, louder, nearer. Say Yes once. That's the leap. Then anchor to your future self. This is the widening. Your future self-tracks receipts: what went right, what you learned, what you'll do again. And what you'll avoid. Then, repeat.

Your job isn't to "feel ready." It's to move yourself forward while your system is still catching up. Expansion doesn't just require courage. It requires capacity to hold yourself steady once you're there. You cannot expand a life that has no direction. You have to actively make yourself bigger each and every day in order to be ready to receive what is already on its way to you.

Identity doesn't arrive with the title; the title arrives with the identity.

Three beliefs the woman you're becoming holds as non-negotiable:

- I'm paid at the level of my impact.
- Visibility is service.
- My calendar reflects my calling.

Three behaviors your elevated self practices weekly:

- One visibility rep
- One BOLD ask
- One capacity investment

Three boundaries your empowered identity enforces

- No-rush work
- No unpaid emotional labor
- No Yes without it applying to my Why.

Practice them now.

SHOW UP FULLY

When you choose to show up fully visible, it's like this release you feel in your body. It's like opening the flood gates. Pouring out everything that has been built up inside of you. You feel grounded. An overwhelming rush of peace and presence. You no longer second-guess your words, your thoughts, or your actions. You no longer question when's the right time. You fully trust in the natural timing of life and the ordainment God has given to you, the assignment you are completing.

When you show up fully, in your wholeness, there's a light that manifests deep within you and it begins to shine through. You invite others to do the same. People gravitate toward you. Opportunities become attracted to you and life aligns in accordance to your say-so. You gain clarity in who you are and who you've always been. Everything in life begins to make sense, and you become this puzzle where the pieces are finally fitting just right. And when you're anticipating the next leap, you view it with admiration and honor instead of fear.

When you show up fully, everything you want in life immediately becomes yours and it's not because of magic or some cheat in the game, it's because you've finally said Yes to you, so the universe has no choice but to do the same. The energy you put out into the world is the energy of readiness, of receiving, of abundance, and that, in turn, is what you receive right back.

EXERCISE: VISION-EMBODIMENT PRACTICE

Here's where we stop talking about who you're becoming and start being her. This isn't just about dreaming—it's about daily embodiment.

Part 1: Embody Her

Grab a journal and think of a time where you felt under-qualified, not ready, or just out of alignment with who you were trying to be. Whether it's a woman who makes six figures, a leader of a thriving nonprofit, or a savvy entrepreneur with her own schedule: take a moment to imagine what that life would look like. How would your days look different? How would you feel once you get there? What is she wearing? What is her demeanor like? How does she carry herself? Visualize it in your mind. Write it down.

Then, ask yourself, "What small step can I take today to feel that way today?"

Part 2: Daily Intention-Setting

Now we're making this a daily practice. Set your intention for the day. Decide who it is you want to be and what you wish to attract. Now, instead of relying on the "need" to receive, reflect on your inner readiness to receive what you desire. Is it a raise? A high-ticket client? A trip to Jamaica? What is your intention?

Are you clutching onto your desires for dear life? Or are you setting yourself up as an overflowing river who is fully capable of receiving more? Start with the inner reality, and the outer reality will catch up to you. You will start to see opportunities you never received before. You will get a random text from someone who was thinking of you, referring a client who would be a good fit, or mentioning a new opening for a position that was never offered before.

Tell yourself every morning that you are her already. And plan an action to do, big or small, that would align with this empowered version of yourself. Try it for yourself.

KEY TAKEAWAYS:
- Your environment shapes your limitations—small containers create small thinking
- Safe goals are actually irresponsible to your potential and impact
- You can do more than you think—your capacity exceeds your assumptions
- Big visions require BOLD action strong enough to overcome comfortable patterns
- Comfort zones expand with practice—each stretch increases your capacity

REFLECTION QUESTIONS:
- What environment or upbringing taught you your current "limits"? Are those limits true or inherited?
- If you could only fail upward, what would your vision become?

- What's the scariest part about succeeding at your biggest dream? (Be honest—success fear is real).
- Who in your life would need to adjust if you started living at full capacity?

Chapter Six
DIM NO MORE

Here's where it gets tricky. You can say Yes, expand your capacity, even embody your future self—and still find yourself playing smaller than your potential. Because expansion without full visibility is just a prettier version of hiding.

Not only was I born BOLD, but I was born into a state that could not match my becoming. I'm from a small town in Rhode Island, the smallest state (no, it's not a part of Boston or Staten Island) with small expectations over who I would be and how far I would go in life. People left New York and Boston to settle for a calmer, more predictable life in Rhode Island. You raise a family, get a good state job, and retire with a modest pension. It was "the life" to most. More like poison to my BOLD, budding brain.

From the moment I could talk, I instantly knew I had to be ahead of everyone else around me if I ever wanted to leave this mundane place. I knew that the situation I found myself in, family members on Welfare and Section 8, high school graduation being the ultimate life accomplishment, and a negligence towards further personal achievement; I had all of the odds against me. The environment I grew up in coupled with a small, subtle state felt as if I was thrown onto the wrong side of the tracks. I had asked God, "Didn't you mean to send me to some place like LA or NY? Surely, you're mistaken here." But little did I know, I would be the first one to make it out of Little Rhody, and I would reach higher heights than anyone I've ever known.

Because I knew I wanted a better and bolder life, I hunkered down into my studies. One thing I knew for certain was that academics took people away from their homes. By the age of 10, I looked my mother in the eye and told her, "I'm going to college and I won't be coming back." Not sure if my 10-year-old self had a certain level of clairvoyance or just plain ignorance at the time, but she definitely had a vision, and that is what carried her through her next 14 years of studies.

I gave my all to school, a lifelong member of the Honor Roll, and AP Princess. I knew I had to get out by any means, and my vision was bigger and bolder than my current situation. I didn't have a role model, a mentor, a predecessor, or a rulebook. I just had a vision and I allowed it to carry me through.

BORN *Bold*

Eventually, I became so consumed with meeting the mark—checking the boxes, reaching the deadlines, getting the A++'s and the 3.8 GPA, going above and beyond— that I started shifting my own sense of worth and value to align with what others applauded me for. Honors Societies. Top 10% in my class. Academic awards and sashes. The lists goes on and on. I was so consumed by carrying out this image of perfection, I began to lose sight of myself in the process.

Then I really started to think: when did my identity become so deeply tied to my degrees, to my titles, and to what I've done? How did I veer so far left from that little girl who was jumping onto platforms in Foot Locker without a care in the world?

I became insecure, uncertain of who I was, and I overthought every decision I made out of fear that I would fail, disappoint, or be judged. I was the glorified academic student, praised for my work ethic and dedication to my studies. No way I could afford to mess up or even be seen trying. I had to execute, and I had to execute well. Without a strand of hair out of place or a page of a book unturned.

THE HIGH-ACHIEVER TRAP

I get it, you think you're the last one who could be playing small. You're a natural leader, a high-achiever (an overachiever, even), highly successful, highly accomplished. But people don't see what I see in you. How you're quick to run a meeting, but question and doubt how your performance was. How you have no problem presenting your latest project in front of your entire company, but are silenced when discussing your own ideas outside of your jurisdiction. How you boast about your accomplishments, but are still waiting on the real move: building out something that is true to you. Something new, innovative, fun, and exciting. Something too scary to say out loud, so you continue to hold off on sharing it with the world.

I see you, boo.

You may do an impeccable job of convincing others that you've got it all figured out, that you're confident, and you know who you are. But I see you. I see past the 20% you allow others to see of you. I see the other 80% that is on reserve, hiding in plain sight, because you're afraid to give people your all. Your authentic self. Your unfiltered, unorganized, unprepared, messy, muddy, real version of you. The one who has gotten this far in life, has done so much, has gotten so far, but still doesn't really know who the hell she is without the titles and the roles. The one who is defined by her role as a mother, what she does for a living, who she provides for, and how much she contributes to society, instead of who she is at her core. And that scares you. That is why you can't make a move.

THE SIX-FIGURE SHAM

In my 24th year of living, just 3 months into my career, I had already been able to score a six-figure corporate job in Queens, NY. I had successfully negotiated my way from a modest post-grad $85,000 salary to a big pimpin'

Born *Bold*

$100,000 salary as a fresh graduate. I was on cloud 9. I strutted into my new job with my Louis Vuitton bag in hand and my cashmere-esque scarf across my chest, acting like I was the shiznit. I had the look, the salary, the nice car, the NY apartment that wasn't just a studio and didn't have rats or roaches. I was living large, lavish, and in charge. Or so I thought.

I scored this salary by boasting on my PT skills, experiences, and confidence (three whole months' worth). And I was actually able to convince several men in high places, with 25 more years of experience than me, that I could handle it. As I showed up to work, filled with excitement and wonder of how I would change the world in the healthcare industry, I quickly was faced with the meager reality. I was onboarded quickly, thrown into the lion's den, forced to assimilate to the high demands of patients on my caseload. I was in way over my head. The scholar? The star pupil? She was drowning. And there was no one coming to save her.

Evaluation after evaluation. The time I was given got smaller and smaller, and my confidence in delivering the best patient care dwindled. Am I doing this right? I asked, without guidance. Is this plan of care appropriate? I pondered without a moment to review or research.

As I gained more and more patients, I learned to ask for help and started to adjust accordingly. Then, I realized more and more patients kept being crammed onto my schedule. Patients with special needs, and patients who were severely debilitated and at risk for falling. I had had enough. Enough putting aside my morals and ethics to satisfy the ravenous need for healthcare revenue demands!

One day, I had been summoned by the CEO of my business. He called me onto a four-way line with his right-hand man and head of HR.

I asked, "What is this about?"

He said to me, "I hear you're having difficulty keeping up with the patient caseload."

"Yes, I've had patients who need one-on-one assistance being double-booked on my schedule and it's just not safe," I replied.

"Well, you new grads come out of school and have this idea that you'll change the world and it's just not realistic. You need to see more patients. That's just life. That's how it works, this is how it's always been and that's how it's always going to be," he hissed.

I felt a huge lump in my throat. My body was shaking with anger and defeat. The fluorescent lights seemed too bright, suddenly, and I could hear my heart pounding in my ears. I knew I couldn't fight back, as this was the company this man had built with his own two hands, and I? I had nothing. I was nobody to tell him how to run his business. I felt powerless. I wanted to say "Screw you, I quit!" but I had dimmed my light, I had given him the power he so craved, and I stood there, numb.

My entire vision of me changing the world, making a difference, transforming people's lives, creating a legacy, all crumbled in one conversation. I went back to work a different me. I had ideas and innovative programs I wanted to bring to the clinic that were never mentioned.

I wanted to shift the way the schedule was to improve patient care and the systems of the business, but I was afraid to speak. I grew resentful, angry, and I felt as if there was a smaller version of me screaming, yelling, and stomping to be set free.

THE COST OF DIMMING YOUR LIGHT

That is what dimming your light looks like in real time. You avoid the spotlight and downplay achievements. You let others take credit for work you poured your soul into. You don't post your wins on social media because "that's bragging." You stay quiet in meetings even when you have the solution everyone's been looking for. You minimize your accomplishments with phrases like, It was no big deal, or Anyone could have done it. You let people interrupt you mid-sentence and never circle back to finish your thought. You take the back seat in photos. You deflect compliments like they're personal attacks because God forbid you accept them—then you have to own up to them.

And the whole time? Your ideas are never brought into fruition. Your impact? Capped. Your legacy? Delayed. All because, like me that day in my corporate job, you decided to shrink. You decided to freeze. You decided to remain quiet. And for that, you're holding off on the very abundant life you deserve. A life of opportunity, grandness, boldness. A life that is full and pure and exciting. You might convince others—even yourself sometimes—that you're content where you are. And maybe part of you truly is. But there's another part of you that knows there's more calling. You have achieved so much on paper, yet there's still something stirring—a vision that feels both exciting and terrifying to name out loud. You hide in the dark, your launches live in the drafts, and that amazing book idea you had at 3 in the morning? Somebody's already published while you were sitting in your indecision of what the cover should look like, without a single word on your manuscript.

You're afraid to be seen trying, failing, and striving for something that doesn't make sense in anyone else's mind but yours. You don't want to seem selfish, you don't want people looking at you like you have three heads when you say you're quitting your corporate job to become a travel blogger. But the truth is, sis, your feelings are valid. Your feelings are not coming from an unknown source. They're coming from the fact that your identity isn't tied to you, it's tied to who you've become and the life that you've created for other people. And it's hard to see you amongst it all.

Here's what's really happening: what might feel like modesty or humility is actually learned invisibility. You've been conditioned by well-meaning messages that taking up space is selfish, that visibility equals arrogance, that owning your power makes you "difficult." These aren't your original thoughts—they're inherited beliefs. You've been taught that being palatable is more important than being powerful. That being liked is more valuable than being respected. That blending in is safer than standing out.

But let me tell you what happens when you keep playing small. Your expertise gets overlooked for someone with half your qualifications but twice your visibility. Your dreams get smaller and smaller until they fit comfortably inside the box others built for you. And one day you wake up and realize you've become a supporting character in your own life story.

THE PINK PROMISE

One cold, rainy day in Providence, Rhode Island back in March of 2025, I was on my way to a funeral. It was for my Titi Olga, who had passed away from a heart surgery that went awry. There, I stared at her beautiful gold and white casket, adorned with white and pink roses, all sad and slouched down, as if they knew this occasion was not one to be joyous for. As I greeted everyone, family, friends, and colleagues, they all said the most lovely words about my titi. She was kind. She was giving. She had dedicated her life to her mother, staying by her side until the day she died. She didn't get married. She didn't have children. In the words of my dear cousin, "Her life was her mom." Everyone admired her dedication, her desire to serve all of her life.

As I sat before her casket, anticipating the moment she would go under and lay within her place of resting, I was furious and frustrated. Tears filled my eyes and rushed out onto my cheeks, where they blended with the rain falling from the sky. How could they be so happy that you didn't get a chance to live, Titi? How could they be satisfied with the life you never got to fully carry out? I pondered. Everyone talked about her mom, what she did for others, but never about her dreams, her goals, her aspirations.

Not once did anyone say, "She had big dreams to become ____ or to do ____," and that made me angry. I felt a sudden sense of responsibility, hope, and promise rush over me. It was as if I felt my aunt telling me I had to create a change. In that moment, I made a promise to my tia that I would help women own their power, say Yes to the dreams and desires they've been holding off on, and activate them to build bigger, bolder legacies.

The workmen began lowering her casket into the terrain, and as my solemn rose was tossed into her place of rest, my promise was sealed along with it. There was no turning back.

My titi Olga did not have enough time on this earth to carry out her dreams, her aspirations, her goals. She didn't have the privilege to think beyond survival and family expectations. You, on the other hand, do. So you don't have to keep performing. You don't have to keep pretending. You don't have to keep striving for the success that you already have. All you have to do is look deep within yourself. The answers lie within you.

You can't make the impact you were designed for from the shadows. You can't change the world with your mouth closed. You can't leave a legacy if no one knows you were here. The world doesn't need another woman who makes herself smaller to make others comfortable. The world needs you at full capacity, full volume, full visibility. The world needs YOU!

EXERCISE: THE VISIBILITY CHALLENGE

For the next seven days, practice taking up your full space:

Day 1: Post one professional win on social media without disclaimers or minimizing language.

Day 2: Speak up in one meeting with a solution or idea you've been holding back.

Day 3: Take credit for something you accomplished when someone compliments you (say, "Thank you, I receive that" instead of deflecting with another compliment back or discredit).

Day 4: Send one email asking for something you want (promotion, opportunity, collaboration).

Day 5: Share your abstract opinion confidently in a group conversation without apologizing for it.

Day 6: Take up physical space—sit at the front at church, speak out loud in a quiet room. Have fun with it!

Day 7: Have one conversation about your goals/vision without stopping yourself for being too ambitious.

Track how you feel at the end of each day and what resistance comes up. Notice the stories your brain tells you about being "too much" or "too crazy." Challenge them with evidence of how your full presence serves others.

> **PRO TIP:**
> Visit www.bornboldbook.com to share about your visibility wins with others to hold yourself accountable!

You don't need to dim your light, you need to reignite it.

KEY TAKEAWAYS:
- Playing small isn't humility—it's learned invisibility that robs the world
- The 80% of yourself you keep hidden is where your real power lives
- High achievement doesn't mean you're not still playing small in key areas
- Dimming your light doesn't serve anyone—visibility is service
- Taking up space isn't selfish—it's necessary for your assigned impact

REFLECTION QUESTIONS:
- In what situations do you automatically make yourself smaller or quieter? What triggers this response?
- What percentage of your true thoughts and ideas do you actually voice? What happens to the other percentage?

- When was the last time you took full credit for something you accomplished without deflecting or minimizing?
- What would change in your relationships if you stopped managing other people's comfort with your success?

Chapter Seven
THE PRICE OF MAYBE

*P*icture this: you go to the meeting. You have an amazing idea that could take the company from good to great, from 30% profit margin to 40%, and just as you're about to raise your hand, you shrink. Your mind starts to flood with negative, limiting thoughts. What if people think I'm dumb? What if nobody agrees? What if my voice cracks when I speak because I'm nervous? So you don't commit to your thoughts, your ideas, your actions. You choose silence. You choose safety instead.

And guess what? Maybe somebody else raises their hand. They say the same idea out loud that you had. Everyone claps, the boss has a big grin on his face, and the recognition all goes to your coworker. She gets promoted to a C-level position with a $20,000 raise. So not only did you miss the recognition for your own genius, you missed the opportunity to grow in your career, to better provide for your family, and to see the impact you can make in the company as a C-suite level leader. The cost has a rippling effect. Not only do you stay small, but the generations before you do, too.

Think about it in the reverse. Say you did raise your hand that day, voice your opinions and ideas, and receive everything your coworker did in the opposite scenario. Now you've got more power, promise, and purpose in the business. So much so that you have the ability to change lives on a global scale, compared to the middle-managerial position you were previously at. Then your daughter sees you in all your glory. She believes in you. She looks up to you and admires how much you've done. How far you've gone. Then she decides she can, too. So she raises her hand in class, even when she is afraid. She applies to Ivy League instead of community college, because she believes she can. She ends up negotiating her salary because she knows her worth and what she deserves. She goes off to change the world, not because you raised your hand in a meeting, but because, in giving yourself permission to be in your power, you subconsciously passed that baton onto her, too.

This same ripple effect made me who I am today. My beautiful mother, BOLD and bright, (though she won't admit it) decided she wanted better for her two young kids living in the south side of Providence. At the tender age of 26, a single mom of two, she left an impossible situation and signed the deed for a new suburban home in the quaint town of Cranston. She went on to pursue not only her Bachelor's, but even her Master's degrees on full scholarship. Traveling over an hour and a half back and forth to Boston, MA every weekend, missing key moments with her growing kiddos, striving to create a better life for them. Because of her grit, I had the launch pad to go further and seek out an even bigger vision, a BOLDer reality.

The consequence of playing small, circling a decision, or avoiding your expansion is greater than losing just what's in the moment. It's telling every little girl around you that they should settle for where they're at, too. It's adding to the systemic oppression that has held women back for centuries now. It's telling the universe, "I don't deserve to grow, to level up, to receive more." And as a result, you don't.

I know I sound tough, but it really is that globally impactful. Your actions today impact the people of tomorrow. Your choices to say Yes to things that scare you are the very keys to unlock doors that were not previously open, but because of your resilience, they are now—and they are wide enough to let the upcoming generation of women follow through. You are the generation who is going to change that.

THE REAL DECISION

You have two choices: submit to society's expectations and let life happen to you, or choose the path less traveled toward something beautiful and unprecedented. My advice? Choose the unknown. Here's how you're going to do it.

Using the O of **The BOLD Method**™ (Own Your Vision), start with this question: What would I do if I had no limitations? Let yourself dream without the voices that say You can't, or You're crazy interrupting.

Allow yourself to dream boldly about the life you've always wanted. Dust off those aspirations you've shelved and bring them to the light. Own this vision like your life depends on it—make it so compelling that it pulls you forward more than the fear holding you back.

Next, embody the woman who has already made the BOLD moves you're contemplating. Be her now, and let that identity guide your decisions.

The next phase of the method is Dominate Your Decision. Decide to take action. Decide that you are no longer waiting. Decide that you are ready for greater, that you are ready for more, that you were meant for more, and you are more than enough to receive it. Decide that you will no longer allow your current situation to define you. Decide that you will no longer allow yourself to be held back from the riches of life. Decide that you aren't gonna let society tell you that you need to conform, that you need to fit in a box, that you need to act a certain way or speak a certain way in order to be accepted.

Decide that the only measurement of your success is how you truly feel about where you're at and who you are. Decide that success cannot be given to you, because it already is living and breathing within you. That is how you make a decision today and I challenge you to, after reading this chapter, make one BOLD decision.

It doesn't have to be packing up all your stuff and moving across the country, but it does have to be big. It has to be audacious. It has to be a little delusional, and definitely all the way out of the ordinary. It has to be a decision that people look to you like you're crazy and ask you if you're all right. It has to be a decision that goes against everything that you've been taught, everything that you've learned from other people, family, friends, coworkers. Something that you would say at a meeting or during a water cooler conversation and receive some intense side eye. Something that burns you up with passion inside and fills you with excitement and fear, all at the same time. Commit to that decision today and execute it by end of day.

Now, execution doesn't have to look like buying a first-class plane ticket or ordering an entirely brand new designer wardrobe, but it does have to look like deciding, declaring and knowing deeply within you that you are all in. So send a text, send the email, set up the appointment, do what you have to do.

Your time is now. Decide to choose you.

> *"Dr. O, you have helped me so much with getting my business started. Coaching with you helped me target what exactly was holding me back from moving forward and identify what I need to do to get my lip gloss business up and running. You helped me with prioritizing myself and finding the confidence to promote my ideas and passions. Before, I was nervous, worried about what others*

would say about me and my lip gloss. Now, I've been at every pop up shop, all over social media, and on the shelves of local beauty supply stores! I went from barely selling a single product to sold out weeks, thanks to you!

You truly have helped me realize that as a mom and business owner, putting yourself first is a good thing even though we're conditioned as women to take care of everybody else, it's okay to say [N]o. Since working with you, my mindset has shifted to realize that once you make a decision for what you want in life, you have to be 100 percent in it. Otherwise, it won't work.

—Jona, previous client

EXERCISE: THE RIPPLE EFFECT DECISION

Think of one decision you've been avoiding that affects not just you, but others around you (family, colleagues, the next generation).

Step 1: Map the Cost
Write down what your indecision is costing:
- You personally (opportunities, growth, income)
- Others watching you (what message are you sending?)
- Future generations (what patterns are you modeling?)

Step 2: Flip the Script

Now write what would change if you made the BOLD choice:
- The doors that would open for you
- The example you'd set for others
- The legacy shift you'd create

Step 3: Make the Call

Set a timer for 24 hours. Within that time, make the decision and take one concrete action step. Send the email. Have the conversation. Submit the application.

Remember: Your courage today creates pathways for the women coming behind you.

KEY TAKEAWAYS:

- Indecision has a ripple effect that impacts generations watching you
- You have two choices: submit to suppression or choose unprecedented expansion
- Making BOLD moves creates pathways for others to follow
- Your courage (or lack thereof) teaches others what's possible
- Decide once, then dominate through consistent action

REFLECTION QUESTIONS:

- What decision have you been researching for months that you could make in the next 24 hours?

- How has your indecision affected not just you, but the people watching you (children, colleagues, friends)?
- What would you choose if "maybe later" wasn't an option and you had to pick "yes" or "no" today?
- What's the most expensive thing you've lost by waiting for perfect information?

Chapter Eight
BREAK OUTDATED NARRATIVES

One time, I was planning on going to Summer Jam with my best friend. Nicki Minaj was going to be there, along with so many amazing artists. It literally was the opportunity of a lifetime. Tickets were on sale at a steep discount, and if I were to buy right then and there, I would score a major win. I held off on buying the tickets, focusing on planning things out with my bestie to meet up, take the train together, and head down to UBS Arena in Elmont, Queens. We picked out our outfits and had the itineraries down to a T. I already saw myself in the crowd, singing my favorite songs, waving my hands in the air like I just don't care and enjoying this concert; the crowd going wild, speakers blaring, and the overarching bliss that waved over the crowd singing in unison. I needed to be there.

When I went to purchase the tickets, they didn't go through the first time. I was shocked, confused. Did I put in the wrong credit card number? Did I have bad Internet connection? I immediately doubted my ability to purchase a simple concert ticket, so I tried again and the same thing happened. "Error loading." "Error." I felt a deep pit in my stomach. Something told me, Onaysia, if it's not meant to be, it's not meant to be. Leave it alone.

Now, I am NOT a woman who takes "No" for an answer, and I'm sure you are too. I will go above and beyond, high and low, against all odds to get what I want. I will try five different credit cards, incognito tabs, different phones, laptops, whatever device I can get my hands on, to make it happen. I will Google everything. I will YouTube and I will research until my eyeballs fall out in order to get what I want. So for me to listen to this voice, for me to lean into what my inner voice was telling me, was huge.

I surrendered. I told my friend, "Hey girl, I'm not gonna be able to make it. I can't get my ticket." We had been planning to go to this concert for months. It was painful to send that text, but something in me knew that something wasn't right. It's like I just wasn't meant to be there, even though my outfit was killer and my plans for the day were magical. I had to let go of what just didn't quite fit.

In the next couple of days, I saw and heard big news about how the Summer Jam ended up getting shot up.

Born *Bold*

A fight broke out, which led to shots firing and punches being thrown. People were hurt, injured in a frantic rage. They scurried left and right, caught in the madness. I thought to myself, Wow, imagine if I was there on that lawn that day. I could've seriously gotten in trouble. Not only could I have gotten potentially caught in the crossfire, but I could've been trampled by the crazy crowds of people running away from the scene. I saved myself from a lot of pain, turmoil, and quite literally just a headache. It was a good thing that I listened to my inner voice and decided to be still, actually take No for an answer.

Sometimes, what you want to hear is not what you need to hear. Sometimes, the move is to wait and listen and be obedient. The more you lean into your inner voice, the more you can fine-tune what its purpose is. Sometimes, it's to keep you safe, and sometimes, it's to be your North Star. You have to learn how to listen. Either way, your inner voice is like your superpower and distinguishes you from anyone else on this planet; it leads you to live a life that is not only aligned, but is BOLDER than you could ever imagine you could be.

OWN YOUR GUT

You've learned to question your gut instincts, to avoid external validation for decisions you already know the answer to. You might find yourself polling trusted friends or advisors, not because you need information, but because you're seeking permission to trust yourself. This pattern of crowdsourcing personal decisions is understandable—and it's also what's keeping you stuck.

This is what happens when you've been trained to trust everyone's voice but your own. When you've been told your feelings are "too much," your instincts are "off," your judgment can't be trusted. When you've been taught that being smart means gathering external input instead of trusting internal wisdom.

The way that you build self-trust is by listening to the inner voice that you have. The voice that tells you to take a left turn instead of a right on your GPS. The voice that tells you to go with the black mini skirt instead of the leather pants. The voice that tells you that maybe you shouldn't keep sleeping because your alarm actually isn't gonna go off again in five minutes, so you should just get up now. The voice that tells you to bring your umbrella even though you haven't checked the weather.

This is your inner voice, your inner guidance, your North Star—it goes by many names. Some may even say this is God speaking to you. The way that you bring this voice back to the surface, or amplify it, is by listening to it and practicing answering to its calling daily. A lot of times, we choose to avoid this voice. We tell ourselves we don't need the umbrella, it's not gonna rain today. Or the GPS says it's to the right, let's go this way. And every time that you choose that, you actively choose to avoid this voice, to neglect it, it shrinks lower and lower and lower until you just don't seem to hear it any longer. That, my friend, is where you never want to be.

This is a part of the B of **The BOLD Method**™: Break Outdated Narratives. Those narratives are built by voices, stories, and beliefs that hold you back. Your voice cannot be heard, because it is so engulfed by the voices of people that you love, or even people who you barely know. It's the voices that tell you, Who do you think you are? when you decide to actually build out that side hustle. It's the voices that tell you, You're not even a good speaker when you decide to lead the team project. It's the voice that tells you that you can't, that you are not capable, that you are not good enough. It's the echoes of your childhood upbringing, when people doubted you or questioned your ability. Or maybe you tried something out, you failed, and you were humiliated, and so now whenever you think about making a decision that scares you, all of those feelings and those voices come flooding back.

You have to dig beyond these voices. You have to excavate your own. You have to get rid of all of the garbage and toxicity and negativity cementing your mind and your spirit. They take you down to the point where you can't even hear your own thoughts. To the point where you can't even speak out of turn without your body cringing.

You've been conditioned so much throughout your life by society, by your culture, by the very people that you love, and it is all intentional. Not all of it is to harm you—some of it is to keep you safe. But all of it is, in fact, holding you back from your greatest potential. And you know that. You know that you were meant for more, and if you keep allowing these voices to keep you where you're at—to hold you in your smallness—you will never get there.

THE FILTER SYSTEM

One powerful, daily tool for self-trust is to use a filter for your thoughts. I don't have any fancy names for it, I just call it like it is. It's when you feel a limiting thought or doubt come into your mind, like maybe if you're questioning whether you should be going after a higher position you don't feel qualified for. And you're feeling those negative thoughts stirring, as they usually do, and you're feeling that urge to click out of the job application and just say, "Forget it."

Ask yourself, Who says I'm not qualified? Maybe it's your competitive coworker. Maybe they believe they're the better candidate, and they make you feel underqualified because you haven't made as much change within the company or lead as many team projects as they have. I say, "So what? So what if you haven't done as much as the next person?"

Filter that thought out and allow a better one to flow in: The only person who can qualify you is YOU!

When you decide that you're taking a step forward on your self-discovery journey, getting to know who you are, and putting yourself first, you're always going to be antagonized by those thoughts. So in order to filter out your mind, you have to challenge those thoughts—daily. These thoughts are either valid or invalid, and where are they coming from?

So the next time the inner voice tells you something, no matter how outrageous or unprovoked or questionable it is, listen to it like your life depends on it. Listen and listen and listen. And when those other voices come, tell them, "Thank you for sharing, but your opinion is not needed here;" then kick them to the curb.

As you continue to listen to your inner voice, it starts to get louder and your vision gets so much clearer. Take it from Chanlee, whose voice had been buried deep for a while until our session:

> *When I first met Dr. Onaysia, I was in the early stages of building my business. I had a story I wasn't sure I was ready to tell. In a small group setting, I finally shared it out loud—and she was there. She listened fully, saw the deeper truth behind my words, and encouraged me to keep going. She told me my story needed to be heard by more people and that my voice could open doors for others, too.*
>
> *That moment gave me the courage to begin sharing more openly and to stop second-guessing my voice. Dr. Onaysia helped me see that my vulnerability was not a weakness, but a strength I could lead with. She sparked the momentum for me to step into a version of myself I hadn't quite owned yet—as a storyteller, guide, and leader.*
>
> *This is what Dr. Onaysia does so well. She doesn't just offer support—she offers reflection, insight, and permission to be fully seen. She meets people where they are and helps them step into who they're becoming. She listens with intention and speaks with clarity. She helps people reconnect with their own wisdom, and she has a gift for helping them show up in a bolder, more authentic way.*
>
> —Chanlee, previous client

EXERCISE: AMPLIFY YOUR VOICE

Spend the next week writing down everything your inner voice whispers to you. Plan out time for meditating, journaling, or sitting outdoors in silence. Allow the voice to come to you, and when it does, write down what it says and DO the action. Then, write down what occurred afterwards. Keep track of the frequency that this voice speaks to you and the positive outcomes that come about because of it.

Practice the daily filter:

1. Who says I can't? - Challenge the negative thoughts/doubts
2. Is this valid? - Trace the thought back to its source and determine its truth
3. What would trusting myself look like? - Act from your own wisdom

KEY TAKEAWAYS:
- Your inner voice is your superpower—it guides you to your unique assignment
- Self-trust is built through practice: make small decisions daily
- External voices drown out internal wisdom—actively excavate your own voice
- Most advice-seeking is really permission-seeking from others
- The filter system sorts valid thoughts from inherited limitations

REFLECTION QUESTIONS:

- Whose voice plays the loudest in your head when you're about to take a risk? What do they typically say?
- What belief about yourself did you inherit from your family or culture that no longer serves your vision?
- When you filter out external opinions, what does your inner voice actually tell you to do?
- What narrative about "people like you" are you ready to personally disprove?

_____

_____

_____

_____

_____

_____

_____

_____

_____

_____

_____

_____

_____

_____

_____

_____

_____

_____

Chapter Nine
OWN YOUR VISION

Courage and boldness often walk hand in hand—one rooted in confronting fear, the other in daring to leap into the unknown. On a seemingly ordinary day, I made a decision that would quietly redefine me: I accepted a travel physical therapy contract in Virginia. But beneath the logistics and paperwork, something deeper stirred. I had long carried a quiet yearning—to live alone, to embark on a journey, not just across state lines, but into myself. After years of dorm floors and shared apartments throughout college, I craved solitude—not as isolation, but as a space to finally hear my own thoughts echo back.

Arriving in Virginia, the contrast was immediate and jarring. Gone were the endless sirens and hurried footsteps of New York City. In their place stood a quieter, slower world—one that felt both alien and full of possibility.

There was lush greenery everywhere. The air was clean and crisp, and there were strips malls and shops right around the corner. It was the perfect balance of city-meets-nature. As I settled into this new environment, something inside me began to shift. I spent my days in Virginia walking on trails, sitting by the lakeside, painting and participating in the arts, living life from a different lens—more full and peaceful. I would journal outdoors in the beautiful Virginia sunshine, and write stories and novels like I did when I was young. I thoroughly felt like I was finally becoming the woman that I had always known, but hadn't taken the time to truly court.

I took myself out on dates. I spent so much more time with me, listening to my own inner thoughts, getting real about my vision and my wants and blocking myself out from anyone else's opinion. My alone time in Virginia became sacred. It changed the way that I saw myself. The way that I saw who I was becoming. I finally stepped into the identity of a full-time coach and business owner. I showed up. I took content creation seriously. I planned out my days. Every Monday, I tried barre classes at the new local gym and spoke to people without being spoken to. I went up to a university and pitched myself to speak and to lead workshops. I pushed myself in ways that I never thought I could, in ways that I was afraid to previously.

But then reality hit. By the time I had to go back to New York City, I was faced with a decision. I had a falling-out with the woman I was renting from and it was time for me to go. My ride would not arrive until five days after the decision needed to be made. I knew I couldn't wait that long, and I couldn't find a train or bus that would get me there. Plane tickets were too expensive, and I really felt like I was gonna have to walk there at that point. Then, as I was sitting there on FaceTime in full blown panic mode, distraught about what to do, my dad asked me, "Why don't you just drive?"

My eyes went wide and I said, "Drive? What do you mean drive? It's eight hours away!" I questioned. Now being from Rhode Island, the most I've ever driven was two and a half hours and that was like going across the country to me. Eight hours meant that I was confined to my car, that I was committed to driving until I made it to my destination, no matter how much I wanted to stop. I couldn't even fathom the thought. I couldn't even believe that he asked me that. The audacity!

THE MOMENT OF TRUTH

I took a deep breath in. I looked around the apartment. I already knew the decision that I had to make, but I was afraid, hesitant, uncertain. The woman I had been becoming in Virginia—confident, self-reliant, BOLD—was now being tested. One thing I knew is that I couldn't stay. I had to go, and because of that fact, I surrendered to my stubbornness. I packed up all my stuff within the hour and headed onto the road.

I told myself, "I can do this. It's just like driving two and a half hours three times." I bargained with myself.

"I'll just stop for coffee and then stop for lunch and then stop again for a potty break. It's fine, it's no rush." But here's what happened: I got on that road and I did not stop until right outside of Jersey. I sat in the car reflecting on my life, reflecting on what I had learned, all the experiences I had gained, what I wanted my future to look like, and before I knew it, I was back in New York City.

I had just driven eight hours! By myself! Without anyone's help! And I didn't have to stop a million times, like I thought I would! I never thought that I could go this far. Literally. I was always the one to ask for help, the one who needed saving, but this time I decided to save myself. I decided to push myself, and when I got to the other side of those eight hours, it was so much easier than my brain was telling me. It was so much more doable than I had anticipated. My ability, my skill set, was better than I expected, and I was sharper than ever. I was filled with pride, filled with joy. I had pushed past my old limits, and as I got to New York City, I was already thinking of my next solo road trip; how much further I could go.

This realization hit me like a wave: the environment I grew up in had shaped my thinking in ways I didn't even realize. Being from the smallest city state in the country, I had these subconscious limitations placed on myself that I wasn't even aware of until I needed to break out of them. And you don't know your own limitations until you are faced with expansion, until you're faced with growth outside of the fishbowl that you grew up in. A snake will only grow to the size of its container, and the same goes for you.

You set goals you know you can hit instead of goals that would stretch you. You play it safe with your dreams because you're not sure you can handle the big leagues. You've convinced yourself that being realistic is being responsible, but really you're just scared to find out what you're truly capable of. You've been trained to settle for what you can see, instead of reaching for what you can become. The whole time, you've been more than capable of getting to the other side of the decision, the move, the leap you've been holding off on.

BREAKING THE CONTAINER

You can do so much more than you anticipate. Your impact is being hacked by your lack of ability to think higher, to think bigger, to think bolder, to think outside of the box that society has placed you in. To be BOLD is seen to be unsafe. To go big is deemed a risk.

What were you told growing up that has shaped you? What aspects of your culture that have limited you? Where do you see this playing out in your day-to-day life?

The more that you allow others to define you, the more that you submit to their expectations of stagnation and settling.

I help my clients raise their goals by eliminating the limitations placed on their minds. The real work is in discovering where these limitations originate. Is the fact that you can't go after a six-figure deal because you are used to having five-figure clients? Or is the real issue that, growing up, you were taught that you can't ask for too much money, and this subconscious thought or belief has then trickled into your adult life, preventing you from more wealth? Once we can tackle the limitations (The B in **The BOLD Method**™), your success rate of taking BOLD action goes up by 96%. The remaining 4% is up to you to decide how to use.

These are the things that cap your goals. They put limits to what is legendary. They try to shrink it into a shape that is molded and defined and smooth when it is more so rigid and uneven and alive and well. In your mind, your vision and your goals are beautifully twisted and not meant to meet the standard. You're a perfectionist, an overachiever, and everything about your vision, the impact you want to make, makes you sick to your stomach because you just don't know how you're going to get there. And so, because you don't know, because you're uncertain, you decide not to share your fullest, most vibrant vision—your truest, deepest desires—because you're afraid that if you say them out loud, you have to commit to them.

PERMISSION TO DREAM BIGGER

You happen to be in luck, because this is what I do. In order to raise your goals, in order to enhance your vision, and in order to do the unexpected, you must be willing to do something different. As the great William Faulkner said so wonderfully, "You cannot swim for new horizons until you have the courage to lose sight of the shore." Let go of what is expected, of what is safe, what is secure—it is all a lie. It is all a means to keep you where you are.

Nothing in this world is secure. Not even your six-figure salary with benefits and 401(k). Social Security isn't going away—but major changes are likely on the horizon. According to the Social Security Trustees' 2025 report, the trust fund could be depleted by as early as **2033**, at which point beneficiaries could face a **23% reduction** in payments unless Congress takes action (bipartisanpolicy.org). And when it comes to the stock market? Despite what we may hope, downturns aren't rare—they happen more often than most people realize. In fact, bear markets (a drop of 20% or more) have occurred roughly every **3.5 years** since 1928, though they typically last less than a year (hartfordfunds.com).

The world is made up of limitless ideas. When the Wright brothers decided that they wanted to fly, everyone looked at them like they were crazy. When Noah was building his ark, I'm sure the entire neighborhood had something to say about it. When NASA shot the first rocket successfully into space—literally out of this world—people had to be shaking in their boots. These are the visionaries that lead the world forward. These are the minds that we need more of. These are the changemakers and innovators making the world a better place.

You are no different than them. You are not crazy, you are not audacious, you're not too much. You were chosen. You have a purpose in this world, and you have to allow yourself to dream big and to dream boldly.

Because if you don't, the dream won't be strong enough to pull you out of your current situation. It won't be magnetic enough to carry you over to the other side. And once you're there, latch on like your life depends on it, and allow it to guide you every step of the way.

Safe goals feel responsible, but they're actually detrimental to your potential. When you aim low, you rob the world of what you could contribute at your highest level. When you play small with your vision, you deny others access to the transformation you could provide. When you settle for less than your full capacity, you betray the assignment you were given.

What would you attempt if you knew you couldn't fail? What goal would you set if you trusted your ability to figure it out along the way? What would you build if you believed you were worthy of massive success? Global change?

Those answers? Those aren't a fantasy. That's your assignment. Dare to dream bigger, bolder, louder. Map out your vision and practice saying it out loud. Share it with a friend, a family member, a colleague. Shout it out to the rooftops! It's your vision to hold!

EXERCISE: OVERCOME YOUR LIMIT

Choose one fear you have: heights, small spaces, bugs. Expose yourself to a small aspect of this fear and go just beyond what you normally can tolerate. The goal isn't to eliminate the fear completely, but to expand your comfort zone by exactly one degree.

Then, apply this same principle to your goals:

1. Identify your current "driving limit" - What's the biggest goal or outcome you think you can handle?
2. Find your container - What environment or upbringing taught you this was your maximum?
3. Plan your 8-hour drive - What would be 3-4 times bolder than your current vision?
4. Take the first mile - What's one small action toward that bigger vision?

Track what you discover about your actual capabilities versus your assumed limitations.

PRO TIP:
Head to www.bornboldbook.com for a list of BOLD vision inspo.

KEY TAKEAWAYS:
- You can do more than your current environment taught you was possible
- Vague desires cannot beat concrete fears—your vision must be compelling
- Environmental limitations become internal limitations until you break the container
- Future-focused thinking expands what you believe is available to you
- Your specific vision exists because you're meant to fulfill it

REFLECTION QUESTIONS:

- What do you want so badly that it scares you to say out loud? Write it down.
- How has playing it "realistic" with your goals actually undermined your capabilities?
- What would your vision become if you removed other people's limitations from the equation?
- If your vision isn't pulling you forward stronger than fear is holding you back, how can you make that vision more compelling?

Chapter Ten
LEAN INTO YOUR FUTURE SELF

Have you ever heard of the phrase growing pains? People love to talk about transformation like it's this graceful, glittery thing—but the truth is, becoming costs something. Take the butterfly. Before it can ever fly, it first has to completely undo itself. Inside the cocoon, it doesn't just rest—it dissolves. It breaks down everything it once was—yes, literally turns itself into mush—before it can become something new.

Then comes the fight. To break free, the butterfly has to push and pull against the very cocoon that once protected it. And here's the hard part: if someone tries to help it too soon—cuts the cocoon, makes the path easier—it dies. The struggle is what pushes life into its wings. Without the fight, the wings never fill.

And even then, after all that effort, the butterfly doesn't soar right away. It hangs there, waiting—dripping, trembling, and still. Until finally, when it's ready, it flies.

Transformation isn't easy. It's not fast. And it's not pretty. But it is necessary. And it is sacred.

When you try something new, something BOLD, something out of the ordinary...your mind will convince you that you aren't good enough. That you aren't ready. That you need more time. That it's not safe. All alarms will go off. All hell will break loose in your nervous system. But this is all meant to keep you safe and keep you small. Growing pains are not only a physical sensation felt within the bones of a young, growing child, or a struggling butterfly. They're an omnipresent feeling that you just can't quite put your finger on. The pain is felt internally, emotionally, spiritually, and mentally. Luckily enough for humans, we don't have to physically break our own tissues down to transform, but we do have to internally shift things around to leave room for growth.

In order to step into your next role, next level, next chapter of your life, you need to let go of a few things. How you think, what you limit yourself to, the habits that no longer serve you. You have to be willing to cut ties with that which reflects your old identity and match it to your new sense of self. You wouldn't order in a brand new, suede memory foam couch without first removing the janky, old one you're replacing. It's just that simple. In order to improve, upgrade, or level up, you have to start with a clean slate and a real assessment of what is no longer serving you.

To emerge as your new and improved self, the You 2.0 if you will, you must struggle. You must break down all the aspects of you that no longer fit. The way you used to handle tough decisions—running, hiding, avoiding—they can no longer serve you. As you elevate into your next evolution of self, the way you doubt your vision and your calling, the way you mistrust that voice in the back of your head that tells you, You're meant for so much more—that can't stay. If you're ready, willing, and have decided that you want your outward life to look differently, you must look inwardly.

Now, I know what you're thinking. But what if I become totally unrecognizable when I change who I am? What then? The answer is: you've always been the woman you're becoming.

Yes, I will say it again: You have always been the woman you're becoming. You're just giving her an exfoliant. A scrubbing of dirty, yucky lies that spoil your brain rotten. A release of generational patterns that hold you back from your highest potential. An oil pulling off the expectations and obligations placed on you by society. Spa days aren't pretty when you've got a bright green mask on, cucumbers for eyes, and your hair wrapped in a rough towel. But the result? Baby. You end up refreshed, renewed, and feeling like a brand new you.

"Beauty is pain." Another quote we hear so often, but we neglect to hone in on its true meaning. Beauty is the emergence of your true self, the you underneath the years of conditioning you have received. And in order to get back to it, you've got to go through some painful things to get there. Your mind didn't become doubtful or fearful overnight. You didn't start playing small after that one kid in sixth grade math class told you you were "ugly." No, your mental jail has been building, brick by brick, as the world continues to weigh down on your genius and your freedom. Not only will you feel pain, but you will feel grief. Grief for who you used to be. Grief for how much you've lost in the process of delaying the life you know you deserve. Grief over losing the woman who no longer waits, no longer asks for permission, and is choosing to be seen, to be heard, to be whole.

HOW TO MOVE FORWARD

Now that you understand why transformation feels like emotional warfare, let's get practical about how to navigate it intentionally. Because feeling the growing pains is just the first part—directing them toward your vision is where the magic happens. The first step to aligning with your future self is to know your vision over your life. And I don't mean the "What's your five-year plan?" type of vision, with the generic corporate climb story and maybe adding in a trip to Oahu, Hawaii. I mean, what's your real, juicy, big, and scary vision that you're even too afraid to tell me (and I'm just writing to you in this book, imagine being in the same room! Forget it!). The dream you've been burying down for years under everyone's "You're crazy"s and "Stick to what you know"s and "Don't take risk"s. The dream you keep yourself from fully carrying out, scared that if it fully manifests inside of your mind, then you'll have no choice but to claim it.

But if not you... then, who? Who will be tasked with carrying out your vision? Who will be passed the baton to do what you couldn't muster up the guts to do? Will it be your daughter? Your granddaughter? Your great-great-great niece? Here's the thing: nobody can bring your vision to life because it is a secret compact between you and God. No one else. That's it. You can't run and hide from divine assignment. You can't pass over your calling like freshly cracked black pepper at Olive Garden. You were chosen for a reason. You were called for a higher purpose. And what you're doing, where you're living, and where you're going is just not cutting it. And I'm certain you're successful, brilliant even. But success does not outperform your soul's assignment.

Once you allow your vision to come to life, it's time you accept it as your assignment. I know you're a scholar, you've got degrees for days. But this assignment here? There is no blueprint. No academic plan. No outline. There are no rules here, just that you commit to placing one foot in front of the other, even when the staircase has yet to appear.

Not all hope is lost, though. I do have another ace up my sleeve.

THE SECRET FORMULA

Now we're getting into the good stuff. The L of **The BOLD Method**™, **Leaning Into Your Future Self.** I promise this isn't another "10X is easier than 2X" psychological hack, or the Five Second Rule that solves all inaction. It's not psychology, and it's not science. But it is real and it does work. Don't believe me? Keep reading.

> *Working with Dr. Onaysia has been truly transformative. She helped me realize that I was sitting on a decision I already knew deep down—I needed to leave my job to create space for myself and my dreams. After just one conversation, she challenged my mindset, held me accountable, and reminded me that BOLD action is the bridge between vision and reality.*
>
> *One of the quotes that stuck with me the most was when she asked, "Why are you so concerned about being a good employee when your goal is to be a CEO of your own company one day?" That moment changed everything for me. Her words gave me the courage to stop shrinking myself for roles that no longer aligned and start building the life I actually want [...] I decided to take action, built out my program, website, and offer, then signed two four-figure clients in just one week!*
>
> *If you're on the edge of a decision, feeling stuck, or doubting your potential—Dr. Onaysia is the person you want in your corner. She doesn't just support you—she calls you forward.*
>
> —Bri, coaching client

You see, what Bri did was something so many people neglect to face. She was operating as her current self: the occupational therapist struggling to start her own business, accepting what others claimed over her life to be the "right thing to do." She was sitting on a decision she already knew the answer to, but could not trust in her vision, nor could she take action towards it.

When you contemplate making a move based on your current skillset, abilities, and track record, your mind will automatically say, HECK NO! YOU CAN'T DO THIS! ARE YOU INSANE? YOU'RE GOING TO MESS UP JUST LIKE YOU DID FIVE YEARS AGO WHEN YOU DID YOUR TAXES WRONG. AND YOU WANT TO RUN A BUSINESS? GET OUTTA TOWN!

When you make decisions based on what you see and feel right in front of you, you will always be faced with a challenge. You will always be faced with judgment, and it will absolutely always come from within yourself.

Being able to align with your future self requires imagination, innovation, and ideation. It requires you to resort back to your BOLD childhood self. It requires you to take your mind back to an untarnished place and to bring that to the surface. Bri eventually became the CEO of an innovative company, pairing her love for children with special needs, her natural skillset as a previous lifeguard, and her experience as a licensed occupational therapist to provide swimming lessons for special needs children. But she couldn't become the CEO version of herself until she first embodied that identity. You have to become the CEO in your mind before the money, before the clients, even before the launch. Everyone thinks it is the other way around. It's not.

As we worked together, Bri began to understand that she already was the CEO of her own company, and that her external world could follow that belief. She was finally able to make the decision to leave her corporate job—not by spiraling, overthinking, or overanalyzing, but by fully embodying her CEO identity, connecting with it, and moving as that empowered woman would move.

Brilliant.

EXERCISE: IDENTITY INTEGRATION RITUAL

Step 1: Define Your Evolution
Write a "before and after" of your identity:
- Who you've been (old patterns, limitations, fears)
- Who you're becoming (new capabilities, mindset, actions)

Step 2: Create Your Transition Ritual
Choose 3 daily practices that anchor your new identity:
- Morning: How does your future self start her day?
- Midday: How does she make decisions under pressure?
- Evening: How does she reflect and prepare for tomorrow?

Step 3: Embody Her Now

For the next 7 days, make every decision from your future self's perspective. Before responding to emails, choosing what to wear, or handling challenges, ask: "What would the woman I'm becoming do right now?"

Track what shifts when you operate from your evolved identity instead of your current limitations.

KEY TAKEAWAYS:

- Identity evolution feels uncomfortable—that's growth, not a warning to stop
- You're not betraying your roots by expanding beyond current circumstances
- Future-self decision-making trains you to become your new identity
- The discomfort of transformation is temporary—the expanded you is permanent
- Some people will resist your growth because it triggers their own stagnation

REFLECTION QUESTIONS:

- What would the woman who has already achieved your goal do differently than you're doing today?
- How would your daily choices change if you truly believed you were already becoming her?
- What identity are you protecting by staying where you are? What would you have to grieve to grow?
- In what small way can you embody your future self's energy before you have her external results?

Chapter Eleven
WHEN BOLDNESS BECOMES A BURDEN

I was once 60 pounds heavier, face filled with breakouts, overworked, and underpaid. We've all been there, right? I was fully focused on bringing my vision—or so I had thought—to life of building out Step By Step Balance Therapy into a household name, changing the way the medical system was set up and transforming thousands of lives. So much so that I had neglected to grab a salad or pick up a weight in what felt like decades. (It was actually just a few months, but let's focus on what matters here.)

As I was sitting in my 450-square-foot office, with four walls, no windows, and my doctoral degree hanging proudly and polished, I sank into my stool with a sort of heaviness weighing on my chest. I had been working 10 hours that day, seeing patients, handling admin work, and planning my next business move. In the midst of this day, I couldn't muster up the strength to look at my laptop. My head was down, I felt exhausted, defeated, and conflicted. What others didn't know was I had the vision I shared with others and my true, deepest, scariest vision underneath my white coat. Hidden so nobody else could tarnish it with their judgmental eyes and second-guessing spirit. I wanted to become a coach, a movement-leader, a brand, and a legacy-leader. It scared me and excited me.

Why do I feel this way? I asked myself.

Then came the whisper: You're supposed to be doing more. It was the Lord speaking to me that day. I felt his stern, yet understanding presence wave over me in that clinic. Worry, doubt, and fear all hit me all at once, like a runner back being tackled by a seven-foot-tall offensive linemen on a football field.

I swallowed hard. Stunned. And a little offended by what the voice had said to me. More?! Don't you see this white coat?! I'm Doing the Thing! Isn't this supposed to be it?

I sat in silence. Listening. Waiting for the voice to respond. It didn't. But it didn't have to. I already knew the decision I needed to make. But, like you so often do, I began to stall and put it off for weeks. Avoiding. Resisting. "Resting."

How could I do it? How could I find the strength to shut down what I thought was my dream life and step faithfully into a new, unknown chapter of my life? To trade the applause of a well-rehearsed path for the quiet, uncertain thrill of carving one of my own?

When I finally got real about what Onaysia wanted, what little Onaysia had always wanted, looking inward instead of outward, and I saw the mismatch between those two things—I knew I had to move. What I truly envisioned was to create a movement that physical therapy just could not take me to. A movement of bad*ss women who don't take No for an answer, don't ask for permission to move, and choose to live out their wildest dreams, BOLDly and unapologetically. Something exercise bands and hot packs were just not aligned with.

THE DISSONANCE

During those 4 weeks prior to shutting down my clinic, I felt out of sorts. I knew I had to make a decision, but I dreaded it. I couldn't fully commit to the decision to shut it all down—but I couldn't stay where I was at. I was facing what many think is an imposter syndrome, but is actually termed identity dissonance.

This is when the negative thoughts get loud: Who do you think you are? You're not qualified for this. You got lucky once, but it won't happen again. Everyone's going to find out you don't know what you're doing. Maybe you should listen to your mom and stay where you are, you have a good job! Don't jeopardize it for a silly dream. That dissonance is your old identity fighting for survival. For years, maybe decades, you operated as someone who played it safe, who didn't rock the boat, who stayed in her lane. That identity served a purpose—it kept you safe, it got you this far, it earned you approval from people who mattered to you. But now you've outgrown it, and it's terrified of being left behind.

So it fights back. It floods your mind with doubt. It reminds you of every time you tried something and it didn't work out perfectly. It whispers that you're being too ambitious, too selfish, too much. It tells you that people are judging you, that you've made a fool of yourself, that you should go back to what you know. It's as if you're headed towards the wrong side of the highway on-ramp and those thoughts are your red WRONG TURN sign, telling you to turn the other way.

Like I did with my clinic, choose to move anyway.

THE DROP: WHEN YOUR SYSTEM CRASHES

Maybe it wasn't shutting down a clinic for you. But you did it. You finally made the BOLD move. You sent the email. You quit the job. You launched the business. You set the boundary. You had the hard conversation. And for a brief, shining moment, you felt unstoppable. You felt like you could conquer the world. You thought, Why didn't I do this sooner?

But now? Now, the high has worn off. The celebration is over. The adrenaline has faded, and you're sitting in the aftermath wondering if you've made a huge mistake. You're second-guessing yourself, feeling regret, maybe even a little empty inside. The voice in your head is getting louder: See? You should have just stayed in your lane, girl.

Welcome to the Post-BOLD Drop. This is the part nobody talks about in motivational content. This is the messy middle between the leap and the landing. This is where most people decide they weren't cut out for BOLD living and retreat back to comfortable smallness.

But you're not most people. You have yourself a certified **BOLDness Coach**™ on your side. And we're going to walk through this phenomenon together.

THE DROP IS REAL—AND IT'S PREDICTABLE

After the adrenaline rush and the big win, your energy crashes. Your body, once riding high on excitement, is now coming down—physiologically and emotionally. It's not a failure. It's recovery.

Just like marathoners feel the "post-race blues" when their dopamine and endorphin surges ease off—even after crossing the finish line—that overwhelming crash is part of the reset (Abbott+1).

Runners often describe it as falling off a "mental cliff"—the elation evaporates, and the body needs time to recalibrate (The San Francisco Marathon).

After I made the decision to shut down my clinic, I felt this overwhelming sigh of relief that I couldn't explain. I had just made the boldest move of my life and I was on cloud nine, filled with optimism and promise. I was on a high.

Then came The Drop. Instead of feeling energized, I felt numb. For weeks, I was worried sick, uncertain whether I had made the wrong decision. Thinking of ways to get my clinic back, give it another shot, and reverse what had been done. Here I was, someone who had been praised for her work ethic, given community citations for her clinical prestige, and looked to as a trusted authority by many. But I couldn't even trust my own decisions.

This is what true, BOLD action looks like in real time: a euphoric high, followed almost immediately by a visceral pull—every bone in your body pleading to retreat. Back to who you were, what you knew, and even those worn-out sweatpants you finally tossed out (because they still are comfy!).

Your job? Stick to the course anyway.

WHY THIS HAPPENS TO BOLD WOMEN
Here's what's really happening during *The Dissonance*.

Your nervous system is hard-wired to resist change—even when the change is positive. It tries to pull you back to what's familiar, because familiarity—no matter how limiting—feels safer than stepping into the unknown (Alexis Ryan, MA, LPCC+2Pattern Breaker+2.)

This is what clinical psychology calls psychological resistance: an internal push-back that arises even when the path forward is clearly beneficial (Wikipedia.) It's not intuition saying you've made a mistake—it's your system recalibrating and defending your current field of safety.

For women who've been conditioned to be the strong one, the reliable one—the one who holds everything together—stepping into something bigger can feel like betrayal. You're not just redefining your identity; you're unsettling everyone who counted on the old version of you. The resulting guilt is real and heavy (Personality JunkieThrive Therapy.)

But here's what you need to understand: this discomfort is temporary. The identity dissonance you're feeling isn't a sign that you made the wrong choice. It's a sign that you made a BOLD choice. It's evidence that you've stretched beyond your previous limitations. It's proof that you're growing.

The women who sustain BOLD living understand that The Dissonance is a normal and anticipated part of the process, not signs they're doing something wrong. They don't interpret these phases as evidence that they made a mistake. They understand that growth is cyclical, not linear. They expect the valleys between peaks. And they choose to move anyway.

NAVIGATING THE DROP AND DISSONANCE

The most important thing you can do during this phase is to be gentle with yourself while staying committed to your new path. This isn't the time to make major decisions or second-guess your BOLD move. This is the time to nurture yourself through the transition.

Physically, your body needs extra care. Sleep becomes non-negotiable. Nutrition matters more than ever. Gentle movement helps regulate your nervous system. You're not being weak—you're being wise. You're honoring the fact that transformation takes energy, and you need to replenish yours.

Mentally, you need to become fierce about protecting your mindset. Limit exposure to people and content that trigger comparison or doubt. This isn't permanent isolation—it's temporary protection while you're vulnerable. Revisit your "why" for making the BOLD move. Read through your receipts and your CEO Vault. Remember what staying small was costing you.

Remember: just because a new space feels uncomfortable doesn't mean you don't belong—it means you're still breaking it in. Like a stiff pair of new shoes, it might feel uncomfortable at first, unfamiliar against your stride. But the longer you walk in them, the more the shoe softens, the more they begin to mold to your shape—until one day, without even noticing, they feel like they were made for you all along.

The Drop and The Dissonance are not your destination—they're your liminal space. You're not stuck here. You're just passing through. And on the other side is a version of yourself who has integrated this growth, who operates from a new level, who has made BOLDness her new baseline.

EXERCISE: DROP AND DISSONANCE NAVIGATION KIT

Create an emergency support system for when the post-BOLD blues hit hard:

For The Drop (Physical/Emotional Crash):
- Recovery Essentials: List 3 non-negotiable self-care practices (sleep schedule, nutrition basics, movement)
- Energy Protectors: Identify what drains you most during vulnerable times (certain people, activities, content)
- Gentle Reminders: Write 3 mantras for low-energy days ("This is temporary," "My body is recovering from courage," "I made the right choice")

For The Dissonance (Mental/Identity Confusion):
- CEO Vault: Review proof that you have made the right choices in the past, which might have felt scary or uncertain
- Remember Your Why: Write one clear paragraph about what staying small was costing you, what your vision is, and how this BOLD move will turn that vision into a reality
- Future Vision: Describe who you'll be once you've integrated this growth

Daily Practice During Both Phases:
- Morning Affirmation: "I am exactly where I need to be in my growth process."
- Evening Gratitude: Name one thing you're grateful you had the courage to change

KEY TAKEAWAYS:

- The Drop is recovery, not failure—your nervous system needs recalibration time
- The Dissonance is your old identity fighting back with intensified doubts
- Physical symptoms after BOLD moves are normal—extra self-care is crucial
- Discomfort in new spaces doesn't mean you don't belong—familiarity develops with time
- Protect your mindset fiercely during vulnerable transformation periods

REFLECTION QUESTIONS:

- What phase are you in right now—The High, The Drop, or The Dissonance? How will you navigate it?
- What support system do you need during vulnerable transformation periods?
- How will you distinguish between intuition guiding you versus fear trying to shrink you back?
- What would you tell another woman going through the same growth phase you're in?

Chapter Twelve
DOMINATE, TAKE ACTION

I want you to understand something: deep in your bones, there is a power that's been quietly waiting—coiled like lightning, hidden beneath the noise of who the world told you to be. You may not have seen it until now. And that's by design.

This world—systems, structures, old stories—wants you tame. Predictable. Contained. It whispers that boldness is dangerous, that ambition must come with permission. That if you wait your turn, maybe one day you'll be allowed to lead.

But you weren't born to wait. You were born BOLD.

What they fear most isn't noise or rebellion. It's your sovereignty—your ability to shift legacies, break cycles, and alter the trajectory of generations. And that kind of power? It threatens the very frameworks that keep you small.

You have your BOLDness.
You have your sovereignty.
You have your ability.
And that combination? It's alchemy. Once you unlock it, the world doesn't just change—it expands. Exponentially. Limitlessly. Like a wildfire of purpose catching light in every corner of your life.

That's my legacy. Helping women see they don't have to wait for a man, a moment, or some mythical milestone to validate their power.

Right now—this moment—you can choose to:

- Launch the company that disrupts your industry, even if your idea started in a journal on a tired Tuesday night
- Break the generational patterns that told you you were undeserving of more: more wealth, more power, more purpose, more impact
- Build movements that create cures for diseases or cultivate spaces for marginalized communities
- Create your own legacy, one that hasn't been outlined and one that pushes past the norms

You can choose to go against the current. Against the mold. Against the boxes, labels, ceilings, and timelines that were never built for you in the first place.

You can choose BOLD. Because BOLDness was never missing—it was just waiting for you to return to it. And now, finally, you have.

Welcome back.

We're at the end of this book, but the beginning of your BOLD life. You've been reminded of who you already are. You've identified what's been keeping you stuck. You've learned to Break Outdated Narratives, Own your Vision, Lean into your Future Self, and Dominate Through Action. You've taken leaps and navigated the aftermath. You've built a blueprint for sustained boldness.

Now comes the most important part: living it.

This isn't about perfection. This isn't about never feeling fear again. This isn't about becoming someone you're not. This is about remembering who you've always been and giving her permission to take up all the space she was destined for. This is about choosing expansion over contraction, visibility over hiding, action over analysis, courage over comfort.

You are not broken. You were never broken. You are powerful, capable, and fully equipped for everything you've been called to do. The only question now is: will you do it?

Will you send the proposal? Will you raise the rate? Will you have the conversation? Will you set the boundary? Will you take the stage? Will you claim the room? Will you own your space? Will you live your assignment?

The world is waiting for your contribution. Your people are waiting for your leadership. Your vision is waiting for your action. Your future is waiting for your Yes.

You've survived the whole cycle now: the resistance, the leap, the high, the crash, the calm. You know what it takes. You've proven to yourself that you're capable of more than you imagined. But here's where most people stop—they treat BOLD moves like one-time events instead of a lifestyle change. The question is: how do you make boldness your new normal instead of your exception?

You've made it this far, which means you've done the work. You've identified where you get stuck. You've named the patterns that keep you small. You've taken BOLD actions and navigated the aftermath. Now it's time to create a blueprint that ensures this isn't just a moment of growth but a permanent shift in how you show up in the world.

Nicole, a CPA-turned-empowerment-coach helping burnt-out professionals shift to blissful lives, is a perfect example of how this shift can literally alter the way you go about life.

> *Through your guidance, I've been able to navigate the twists and turns of leaving corporate life and stepping into entrepreneurship, confronting and overcoming limiting beliefs that once held me back.*
>
> *Because of your impact, I now trust myself in ways I never imagined, and I've gained the courage and boldness to go after what I want—believing I am worthy of it. By witnessing how you consistently show up in the world—with authenticity, resilience—I've not only learned, but also found the space to rise above challenges and embrace my own power.*

> *Dr. O, you have shown me—and countless others—that true leadership is not about titles, but about creating lasting impact. Because of you, I no longer question my path or the legacy I'm building; I live by it. Faithfully and fully.*
> —Nicole, previous client

THE ANCHOR PHASE: BUILDING YOUR FOUNDATION

After the Drop and Dissonance comes The Anchor phase. This is where you implement routines and practices that help you stabilize. You stop relying on feelings to guide your actions, and start relying on systems. You create structure that supports your new identity instead of hoping motivation will carry you through. This is where the real work happens—not in the moment of the BOLD move, but in the daily practices that make the new level sustainable.

For me, this looked like taking three sabbaticals to get right with myself. I had to create completely new routines around nurturing my body, my mind, my soul. I had to learn to listen to my own voice again instead of constantly seeking everyone else's approval. I had to build daily practices that reinforced who I was becoming instead of who I had been.

You need anchor habits that keep you tethered to your new identity when your feelings are telling you to retreat. You need systems that support your growth when motivation is low. You need practices that remind you why you made the move when old patterns are calling you home.

Personally, I surround myself with other people who reflect where I'm going—not where I've been. Only people who remind me of my BOLDness, my ability, and my sovereignty. You have to be very protective of your energy like your life depends on it. Like it's the last cookie in the cookie jar. You have to block off any and all negative forms or forces that are formed against you. Otherwise, you will block your blessings as well as your BOLDness. Be careful what you listen to, what you see on social media as you're scrolling, what pages you follow. Do a detox of all of the input that you have coming your way. Really ask yourself: is this a reflection of who I have been, or who I am becoming? And allow your environment to anchor you. To reflect back who it is that you've become and are continuing to evolve into.

Another habit I've formed to anchor myself is to practice affirmations in the mirror every morning. What started off as a simple, "Love you, girl," developed into a full-blown daily power shift. Not only do I tell myself how much I love myself, I tell myself that I am good enough. I tell myself that I am good at what I do, that I'm transformational and powerful and amazing and that I am on the right path. You have to continuously remind yourself of that, because you don't have a professor to give you an academic plan and say you only have three credits left until you complete this degree. It's entirely different, because you are going to limits that no one else you know has been, and even your closest allies may eventually fall off because they can't see your vision and they don't understand you. And so you have to be the one to have your own back. You have to be that steady support system that anchors yourself. You have to be your own bestie, cheerleader, and coach, all in one.

YOUR BOLD BASELINE

Eventually, you settle into your new self. The new level starts to feel normal instead of foreign. Your confidence becomes a deep inner knowing instead of a loud, boastful claim. You stop celebrating basic things and start setting your sights on the next growth edge. This is when you know the transformation has really taken hold—when what used to feel impossible now feels like a regular Tuesday.

This is what I want for every woman in this world to experience. Every woman who is sitting in a corporate room, looking out the window and watching life pass by as she sits in her "What ifs" and her "Maybe somedays." There's so much out there in the world you are meant to have. You were placed on this earth to receive everything that it has to offer, and it's time that you claim your inheritance.

The women who came before us worked too hard for you to settle for the mundane. They worked tirelessly for hours, sweat on their backs, being underpaid, underserved, and overlooked. Our grandmothers didn't have the choice, the luxury, the opportunity to dream because they were so worried and fixated on what food was going to be placed on the table and how they were going to survive.

My grandma used to sell hotdogs and piraguas (snow cones) on the corner of Delancey and Eldridge in the Lower East Side of Manhattan for hours in the hot New York City sun, alongside her mom. She didn't have time to think about her dreams, her vision, her aspirations. She just knew she needed to help her mom feed her family, and that was the extent of where her mind could go.

We get to think differently.

We do have that luxury. We do have that ability to be whoever we want to be, to become whatever we want to be. That opportunity is not only a privilege, but it is an honor. And the way that we honor the struggles of our predecessors is to own our power, and know that we have been given permission by those who came before us, by those who paved the way for us to escape the fight or flight, the survival cycle, the feast or famine that our families have faced for generation after generation. It is time that you break your generational curses. It is time that you be the torchbearer of your own legacy. It is time that you put an end to our suffering as women of color. You have the power to do that. You have the power to make change that has such a ginormous rippling effect that it will be felt by your great-great-great granddaughters.

You are the changemaker, the way maker, and God has equipped you with everything that you need in order to make it happen. That sign, that whisper, that feeling within you, it is there for a reason. You feel as though you were made for more because you were. God says you are fearfully and wonderfully made (Psalm 139:14 (NIV)) and it is true. Believe it, embody it, stand in it. Remember your BOLDness. Remember who you were before the world told you who you had to be. Remember everything that you had available to you, how your imagination ran wild when you were young, and how you ran around in the backyard in the grass barefoot without a care in the world, never doubting who you could be—a doctor or a lawyer, an astronaut, a hairstylist. Call that BOLDness forward and allow it to equip you, to prep you, to sustain you, as you go after everything life has to offer you.

EXERCISE: YOUR BOLD OPERATING SYSTEM

Create sustainable systems that make boldness your baseline, not your exception.

Step 1: Anchor Habits (Daily)
Choose 3 non-negotiable daily practices:
- Identity reinforcement (affirmations, visualization)
- BOLD action (one decision that moves you forward)
- Energy protection (boundaries around input/environment)

Step 2: Growth Challenges (Weekly)
Set weekly stretch goals:

- Monday: Make one ask that feels uncomfortable
- Wednesday: Share one idea/opinion you've been hiding
- Friday: Take one action toward your biggest vision

Step 3: Legacy Moves (Monthly)
Plan monthly BOLD moves that create lasting change:
- Month 1: Announce something publicly
- Month 2: Invest in your expanded identity
- Month 3: Make a move that impacts others

Step 4: BOLD Accountability
Share your operating system with someone who will hold you accountable to showing up at this new level consistently.

KEY TAKEAWAYS:
- BOLDness is a practice requiring daily systems, not just personality traits
- The Anchor phase builds sustainable transformation through consistent routines
- Your courage breaks generational patterns and creates new possibilities
- Success isn't about perfect execution—it's about persistent movement
- You honor previous generations by fully using the opportunities they created

REFLECTION QUESTIONS:
- What BOLD move are you ready to make that will create a ripple effect for the women watching you?
- How will you anchor these new patterns so they become your baseline, instead of your exception?
- What legacy do you want to leave through your willingness to live boldly?
- What's the first BOLD action you'll take in the next 48 hours to prove to yourself that transformation is real?

Epilogue
YOUR BOLD ACTION PLAN

This is about building a life where boldness becomes your default instead of your exception. Where taking up space feels normal instead of scary. Where asking for what you want is automatic instead of agonizing. Where setting boundaries is natural instead of negotiable. Where visibility feels like second-nature instead of self-sabotage.

The women who truly transform don't just make BOLD moves—they become emBOLDened. There's a difference. Making BOLD moves is about individual acts of courage. Becoming BOLD is about rewiring your identity so that courage is your default setting. It's about building systems and practices that support expansive living even when expansive living feels uncomfortable.

BREAK OUTDATED NARRATIVES (ONGOING): INTERRUPT OLD PATTERNS

Your job is to catch yourself in the loops before they spiral. Track every moment you catch yourself in overthinking, perfectionism, or delay tactics. Note what triggers send you into analysis mode instead of action mode. Practice the 2-minute rule: if it takes less than 2 minutes, do it now. Use the 24-hour decision rule for anything you've been circling for more than a week.

OWN THE VISION (DAILY): CLAIM YOUR DIRECTION

Write your vision in present tense, as if it's already accomplished. Keep your vision at the forefront where it is always accessible to you. Bring it forward daily using your vision board and future-self visualizations. Practice vision-based responses to opportunities: "Does this serve my vision?" Start using language that reflects that vision: "I am" instead of "I want to be."

LEAN INTO YOUR FUTURE SELF (WEEKLY): EMBODY THE NEXT LEVEL

Make one decision from your future self's perspective. Dress like your future self. Speak like your future self—confident, clear, no unnecessary qualifiers. Set boundaries like your future self. Network like your future self. Practice receiving like your future self. Create an environment that supports your expanded identity.

DOMINATE. TAKE ACTION. MAKE THE LEAP (MONTHLY): LOCK IN THE NEW LEVEL

Make major announcements about your next level. Take actions that make your growth public and irreversible. Ask for things you couldn't have asked for before. Connect with people who represent your next level of growth. Invest in things that support your expanded identity.

Find someone you trust to hold you to your BOLD ideas. Tell someone your audacious idea to start a dog grooming mobile business and ask them to check on you by a certain date to make sure you hold your end of the bargain. Then you're going to go back to Owning Your Vision and allow this to be at the front of your mind at all times. Never let that vision go, and if you start to feel it fade, start journaling as the woman who has already Done the Thing.

EXERCISE: FUTURE-SELF JOURNALING

Write in the current present tense about what will happen. For example, write today: "My business is thriving. Today I have three dog clients, and I spend my morning shaving Mr. Winston, who was a wiggly little guy and just wouldn't let me get the shaver close enough to his fur. Then I went home and did some copywriting for my advertisements, went for a walk, and had spaghetti carbonara for dinner. It was an amazing day. I feel like I'm really starting to get this business going."

This is a foolproof way to fully embody the L of the BOLD, Lean Into Your Future Self, and to ensure the life you want is not only a fading desire, but a cemented certainty. As you are writing the stories in your journal, feel the words as if they have already been done. Feel what you would feel as if you were in that moment now. And the more that you practice this, the more that your actions will align with it, and then your outcomes will be the same. Your thoughts will turn into your beliefs, your beliefs will drive your actions, and your actions will direct your outcomes.

EXERCISE: THE 90-DAY BOLD MOVES MAP

Map out your specific BOLD moves for the next 90 days:

Month 1: Plan Strategically and BOLDly
1. Look at your 12-month calendar year and identify 3 major moves you could partake it that will completely transform your world today.
2. Schedule out each move at the beginning of each month. You'll be collapsing your 12-month timeline into 3.
3. Build in daily and weekly anchoring practices that lock in your vision and anchor you to the future

self who has already achieved these goals. Track your progress daily.

Month 2: Assess Your Advancement
1. Identity ways in which you've shrunk back to old ways, thinking, and tendencies. Name them and cross them out. Swap them for that which reflects the identity of who you're becoming. Your BOLDest self.
2. Get your accountability partner. Share your deadlines and invite them to do their own version of this sprint with you. Check in with them weekly. Do not change the dates.

Month 3: Embrace Your BOLD
1. Make a list of all wins, big and small, that you've accomplished along this journey. Share how much you've achieved with your email list, friends, and family. Celebrate YOU!
2. Rest. Realign. Recuperate. You've done A LOT. Now it's time to give back to you before you set off to make your next BOLD move. Take 2–4 weeks off, then repeat.

The world needs you at your fullest capacity. Not just on good days, not just when you feel confident, not just when conditions are perfect. The world needs you to show up fully, consistently, unapologetically. Your voice matters. Your vision matters. Your contribution matters. But only if you keep showing up to deliver it.

You're already BOLD. You've always been BOLD. Now it's time to be BOLD out loud. Let the world see you, the real you.

It's time to move.

The revolution starts with you.

Not tomorrow. Not when you feel ready. Not when the conditions are perfect.

Today.

Every woman who has ever changed the world started exactly where you are right now—with a choice to stop negotiating with smallness and start living up to the bigness of her assignment.

Your great-great-granddaughter will either thank you for the pathways you created, or wonder why you had all the tools you needed to act, but never truly utilized them.

Which story will you set in stone? Which legacy will you choose to carry forward?

The woman holding this book—*you*—she's done waiting for permission. Done dimming her light. Done shrinking herself to fit inside ceilings that were never built to contain her.

And when a woman chooses to be BOLD, the world trembles. Her light does not just shine—it floods, ignites, and sets fire to every playbook that once told her No.

From this moment forward, the world will never be the same. And neither will you.

Your BOLD life isn't waiting in the distance. It's been here all along. Waiting for you to claim it.

Now.

Is your time.
To.
Be.

BOLD.

YOUR NEXT BOLD MOVE

If this book has stirred something in you, if you're feeling the call to step fully into your power, if you're ready to stop playing small and start living boldly, I want to work with you personally.

This is where the real transformation happens—not just reading about boldness, but activating it in real time with support, accountability, and a coach who won't let you shrink back into old patterns.

Book your Boldness Audit, where we'll identify exactly what's keeping you stuck and create a personalized action plan to break through to your next level. This isn't about motivation—it's about activation. This isn't about inspiration—it's about implementation.

Your BOLD life is waiting. Let's build it together.

Scan the QR code below, or go to <http://bornbold-book.com/> **and let's get to work, together.**

ABOUT THE AUTHOR

Dr. Onaysia Martinez—widely known as *The Bold Coach™*—is a published author, dynamic speaker, and transformational coach committed to helping women activate the boldest version of themselves. A graduate of American International College, she holds a Doctorate in Physical Therapy along with extensive training in psychology, equipping her with the unique ability to "hack" her clients' minds and move them into decisive, life-changing action.

Through her signature **B.O.L.D. Method™**, Dr. Martinez flips traditional coaching on its head. Her clients experience immediate transformation—within just 90 minutes, women have quit corporate jobs, launched six-figure businesses, and set off to travel the world—all by choosing bold action over hesitation.

Her own journey is proof that boldness works. Fired from corporate for refusing to stay silent, she launched a thriving clinic within three months of licensure. And when that success no longer aligned with her vision, she boldly walked away to dedicate her life to empowering women to break invisible ceilings, collapse timelines, and create legacies they once thought impossible.

For more information on coaching, programs, and events, visit **www.bornboldbook.com**.

Works Cited

Abbott. (2023, April 4). *Post-Race Blues: The Neuroscience of Marathon Recovery.* Abbott Health News. Retrieved from https://www.abbott.com/corpnewsroom/nutrition-health-and-wellness/post-race-blues-the-neuroscience-of-marathon-recovery.html

Alexis Ryan Therapy. (2024, August 20). *The Familiarity Factor: Why We Struggle with Change.* Retrieved from https://www.alexisryantherapy.com/blog/2024/8/20/the-familiarity-factor-why-we-struggle-with-change

Baumeister, R. F., Bratslavsky, E., Finkenauer, C., & Vohs, K. D. (2001). *Bad is stronger than good.* Review of General Psychology, 5(4), 323—370. https://doi.org/10.1037/1089-2680.5.4.323

Gilligan, C. (1977). *In a Different Voice: Psychological Theory and Women's Development.* Harvard University Press. (Referenced via Personality Junkie)

Hanson, R. (2009). *Hardwiring Happiness: The New Brain Science of Contentment, Calm, and Confidence.* Penguin Random House.

Hartford Funds. (n.d.). *Guide to Bear Markets.* https://www.hartfordfunds.com/practice-management/client-conversations/managing-volatility/bear-markets.html

Hershfield, H. (2023, July 24). *Becoming Friends with Your Future Self.* Psychology Today. https://www.psychologytoday.com/us/blog/between-cultures/202307/becoming-friends-with-your-future-self

McQuiston, B. (2025, July 25). *Enjoy Your Post-Race High, Deal with Post-Race Blues & Learn All About Post-Race Recovery.* The San Francisco Marathon Blog. https://www.thesfmarathon.com/blog/2025/07/25/enjoy-your-post-race-high-deal-with-post-race-blues-learn-all-about-post-race-recovery

MIT Media Lab. (2024, June 5). *AI Researchers Build 'Future Self' Chatbot to Inspire Wise Life Choices.* The Guardian. https://www.theguardian.com/technology/article/2024/jun/05/ai-researchers-build-future-self-chatbot-to-inspire-wise-life-choices

Personality Junkie. (n.d.). *Women Know Themselves Relationally.* https://personalityjunkie.com/07/women-know-themselves-relationally-connected

Psalm 139:14. *Holy Bible, New International Version.* "*I praise you because I am fearfully and wonderfully made; your works are wonderful, I know that full well.*"

Scientific American. (2012, August 10). *How Does a Caterpillar Turn Into a Butterfly?* https://www.scientificamerican.com/article/caterpillar-butterfly-metamorphosis-explainer

The Well-Being Collective. (2023). *Your Nervous System Will Always Choose a Familiar Hell Over an Unfamiliar Heaven.* Medium. https://thewell-beingcollective.medium.com/your-nervous-system-will-always-choose-a-familiar-hell-over-an-unfamiliar-heaven-e52a71d57803

Thrive With Therapy. (2025, May 20). *You Were Always Good Inside: Healing from the Good Girl Identity.* https://www.thrivewiththerapy.com/therapy-blog/you-were-always-good-inside-healing-from-the-good-girl-identity

Wikipedia Contributors. (2025). *Psychological Resistance.* In Wikipedia. https://en.wikipedia.org/wiki/Psychological_resistance

Yang, Y. (2024). *The Effect of Future Self-Continuity on Intertemporal Decision-Making.* Frontiers in Psychology. https://www.frontiersin.org/articles/10.3389/fpsyg.2024.1437065/full

ZME Science. (2023, May 8). *How Caterpillars Gruesomely Transform Into Butterflies.* https://www.zmescience.com/feature-post/natural-sciences/animals/invertebrates/how-caterpillar-turn-butterfly-0534534

www.ingramcontent.com/pod-product-compliance
Lightning Source LLC
Chambersburg PA
CBHW052100230426
43662CB00036B/1718